Stewards of the Mysteries of God

Stewards of
the Mysteries of God

Edited by
ERIC JAMES

Foreword by the Bishop of St Albans

Darton, Longman & Todd
London

First published in 1979 by
Darton, Longman & Todd Ltd
89 Lillie Road, London SW6 1UD

© Eric James, 1979

Printed in Great Britain by the Anchor Press Ltd
and bound by Wm Brendon & Son Ltd, both of Tiptree, Essex

ISBN 0 232 51432 1

Contents

Foreword

In its worship, thought and expression, the Church too often presents a face which is more banal than blissful. We are too often the Church of the scribes, the learned and sensible who fail to do justice to the mysteries which elude the clever and the men of common sense. This book signposts the mysteries for us, not the wordy pseudo-mysteries of secret societies and esoteric cults but the inexhaustible yet homely mysteries of divine and human existence revealed in the life and death of Jesus Christ.

In this realm we rapidly come into the language of paradox, and a bishop's safest eloquence is silence. Let me just express on behalf of the Diocese of St Albans my thanks to Canon Eric James for having led our thoughts in this fruitful direction and to the distinguished team which he has gathered to contribute to this book. I can heartily commend these essays as the kind of equipment we need to fulfill that particular calling of the Christian life which is

> 'to take upon's the mystery of things,
> As if we were God's spies.' (*King Lear*)

Robert St Albans

Introduction by the Editor

This book began with a particular event and its preparation: a Conference of the clergy of the Diocese of St Albans which is held every three years, this particular conference to take place at the University of Kent, Canterbury, in September 1979. We had chosen for the Conference the theme that is the title of the book.

It is a great theme; and unless those coming to the Conference gave some thought to it before the Conference it was unlikely it would receive at the Conference itself the profound attention it deserves. So, in one way, this is simply a book to prepare three hundred clergymen for a Conference. Yet these days no one can be entirely happy with such a gathering of clergy closeted together by themselves, without some attempt to share with others what they are receiving. There seemed everything to be said, therefore, for making at least our preparatory work available to the people of the parishes of the Diocese. And why keep to ourselves as a Diocese what has been so generously prepared for us by people from, in the main, outside our Diocese on so important a theme? (And our sharing is not entirely without self-regard: how could we afford to produce a book like this for ourselves alone?)

The Triennial Conference of the Clergy of the Diocese of St Albans has always been a particular responsibility of the Canon Missioner, and I gladly accept responsibility for pressing upon the Bishop and his staff that 'Stewards of the Mysteries of God' should be our Conference theme.

The conviction that this should be the theme came to me in a particular way. I had been browsing through the shelves of

1

sermons in the library of Verulam House, our retreat and conference centre in St Albans. There was at least a score of sermons on 'Stewards of the Mysteries of God'. Almost without exception they were sermons preached at ordinations over the course of a century or more. What was said was virtually the same in each sermon. It is ordination which makes a man a minister of Christ and a steward of the mysteries of God, for it makes him a minister of God's word and sacraments. I searched in vain for a single sermon that says that one of the main tasks of those ordained is to help those *not* ordained to be ministers of Christ and stewards of the mysteries of God.

If this is what people have been taught for a century and more, small wonder that the clergy do not find it easy to adjust to a wider conception; that ordinary men and women feel left out; and that the world of work and politics and science, for instance, is spoken of so often as outside the realm of the 'mysteries of God'. Prayer and preaching, worship and bible-study come within that realm; not much more. It seemed, therefore, urgently important to look at the phrase again.

The incident of the sermons, in fact, only focused and sharpened what had been a growing conviction: that the time is ripe—and the world is ripe—for a new understanding of the 'mysteries of God'. In an odd, paradoxical way the interest of young people in the Devil confirms that—and so does, for instance, the popularity of religious paperbacks. The institutional Church may not be attracting hordes of new converts, but in the last decades there has been a new and not simply surface interest in religion, a concern that is not far from concern for 'the mysteries of God'. But it is not to the ordained that people turn first of all as the chief stewards of those mysteries—not, at any rate, to the ordained of the Church of England. The thousands, for instance, who fill the Royal Albert Hall night after summer night for the Promenade Concerts are not deaf, surely, to the mysteries of God. Or those who read Tolkien and *Watership Down*, and many a modern novelist.

One steward of the mysteries of God for me has, in fact, been the leading Australian novelist, Patrick White, ten of

2

whose novels are now in paperback.[1] Dr Peter Beatson has published a major study of his work, *The Eye in the Mandala. Patrick White: A Vision of Man and God*.[2] In White's work, Beatson says, 'the familiar is fused with the strange to transform the map of Australia and the topography of the inner life into a realm of myth. That which is known and rational is used in the service of the unknown and the non-rational.' There is 'a religious pattern that underlies his artistic universe'. His writing is 'an attempt to revivify certain theological clichés and to reveal their contemporary relevance'.

Every aspect of the world of experience bears His signature. Every encounter in the human and natural worlds is potentially a moment of dialogue between the individual and God. A strong current of Grace flows through the universe, which may be experienced ... as the spark of divinity placed in the heart of man ... in the beauty and terror of the natural world.... It is strongly suggested in all the books that a man may achieve union with the One, but this is only reached through a lifetime of encounters with a series of Moment Gods, between which encounters, vast tracts of desert must be crossed. It is his experience of the desert, as well as of the moments of Grace, that finally brings man to salvation. So Patrick White's central subject is not the Hidden God but the Incarnation. His novels are an attempt to inject new and urgent meaning into the almost moribund theological doctrine of 'the Word made Flesh'.

An editorial introduction is not the place for an extensive study of a novelist. But it is worth quoting some of White's own words in which he explicitly states his aim as a writer:

I suppose what I am increasingly intent on trying to do in my books is to give professed unbelievers glimpses of their

1. Patrick White, published by Penguin Books.
2. Peter Beatson *The Eye in the Mandala. Patrick White: A Vision of Man and God* Paul Elek 1976

own unprofessed factor. I believe most people have a religious factor, but are afraid that by admitting it they will forfeit their right to be considered intellectuals. This is particularly common in Australia where the intellectual is a comparatively recent phenomenon. The churches defeat their own aims, I feel, through the banality of their approach, and by rejecting so much that is shocking and sordid which can still be related to religious experience. . . . I feel that the moral flaws in myself are more than anything my creative source.

Peter Beatson uses a quotation from Simone Weil to illustrate what he thinks lies at the heart of Patrick White's work:

In order that a new sense should be formed in us which enables us to hear the universe as the vibration of the word of God, the transforming powers of suffering and of joy are equally indispensable. When either of them comes to us we have to open the very centre of our soul to it, just as a woman opens her door to messengers from her loved one. What does it matter to a lover if the messenger be polite or rough, so long as he gives her a message?

It was the sense that the novelist is often the steward of the mysteries of God that made me want to have a novelist as one of the contributors to this book. Quite recently, for instance, I had read a novel on that mystery of God, bereavement, in which the author seemed to understand as in no other novel I had read before what it is to be totally bereft as a young widow; how different people react so differently towards the reality of death; and the calm, unselfish compassion which can sometimes—in time—reclaim from his private purgatory someone who has been bereaved. Here certainly, I thought, is a steward of the mysteries of God. I therefore plucked up my courage and wrote a careful letter to the author, inviting her to be a contributor to this volume.

The reply I received was disturbing and painful. She said she could not possibly make the contribution I asked for. The phrase didn't mean anything to her; indeed, it was quite meaningless and odd, 'like so many such phrases which serve to make the Christian churches and doctrines quite impenetrable to most people'. Perhaps, she conceded, it would mean much to professional theologians, or to those 'brought up on the jargon'. But, she insisted, she was not any sort of 'orthodox or church-oriented believer' and would feel it quite wrong to try to pretend she was, by attempting to wrestle with St Paul's 'curious expression'. She agreed there was a need to 'come to terms with mysteries'—for everyone to do that; but she couldn't go further than that, 'except in so far as I might have done so—though not deliberately—in writing fiction'.

That writer of fiction would, I am sure, be furious if, after all she had conscientiously said, I should make her out to be a believer in spite of herself. And yet, that letter made me certain of one thing: that many will say with a passionate astonishment, '*When* were we stewards of Your mysteries? We've never been or done any such thing.' But He will say: 'Inasmuch as you have wrestled with what it means to be bereaved in the way *you* have wrestled with the mystery of bereavement—and comforted the bereft in the way that *you* have comforted the bereft—I tell you you have been a steward of My mysteries.'

That letter made me think a good deal more about those whom I should ask to contribute to this book; but it also made me envisage a volume that might succeed this one—after the Conference is over, so to speak—one which put the question to a number of people in different walks of life and of quite different experience: 'What are the mysteries of God for you? Who in your life so far have helped to unveil them—to steward them?'

Yet even in this volume it seemed important to have not only a biblical theologian but also a poet, and a lay theologian as well as a priest; not only a parish priest but one who is involved in the day-to-day life of the social services in the inner area of a great city. It seemed important to ask someone to try to see beyond the surface of unbelief in the mysteries of God.

Working away at the book—and at its title phrase—has convinced me that the heart of the phrase is that word 'mystery'. We are not stewards like race-course stewards or club stewards who are in charge of something that is handleable and manageable. We all of us have not only to keep on going back to the word—and let it take charge of us—we have to go on confronting and allowing ourselves to be confronted by *the mystery of God*. Hence I have included with particular gratitude seven meditations on one of the great mysteries in the life of Christ, the Transfiguration. Dr Eric Abbott encourages us to be silent before the Mystery of the Transfiguration much as my anonymous novelist taught me to be silent—as she herself had clearly been silent—before the mystery of bereavement.

In the Père Marquette Lecture for 1970 'Mystery and Truth' (which, had it not already been published in his book *Thinking About God*,[3] I would dearly have wished to include with the other contributions to this volume) Professor John Macquarrie has this to say:

> There is today a revival of interest in mystery and of the sense of wonder in our secular society, especially among young people. This may mark the beginning of a revulsion against the long established hostility to mystery in Western philosophy. Now if it is true that the most natural (though not the only) way into mystery is through the exploration of man himself, then the Christian faith is singularly well situated to give a lead in the quest for mystery. By its doctrine of the incarnation, Christianity holds that it is precisely in a human person, Jesus Christ, that the final mystery of being has been opened up. According to Paul, Christ is 'the revelation of the mystery which was kept secret for long ages' (Rom.16.25–6). This is commonly taken to mean that Christ has revealed or opened up the mystery of God. But would it not be correct to say that he has done this by opening up the mystery of man? Is there not a deep affinity between the mystery of God and the mystery of humanity? By becoming man in the fullest sense, that is to say, in a measure of fulness that transcends all our ordinary levels of manhood, Christ manifests God in the flesh. He pushes

3. John Macquarrie *Thinking about God* S.C.M. Press, London 1975

back the horizons of the human mystery so that they open on to the divine mystery, but he does this without ceasing to be man.

In the end, that is what this book is about. It is certainly not primarily about the role of the clergy. But it will be clear from this volume that the clergy have to continue to work at the painful task of rethinking their role in society—and they cannot do that by themselves. To confront at any fundamental level the question of the role of the clergy in society is in fact inescapably to confront the 'human mystery'.

Can the mystery of man be preserved without special places and times and people concerned with that mystery? Or does the preservation of such places and times and people 'set apart' magnify the task of enabling us to see the Mystery in all places, all times, all people? Does, for instance, a clerisy all but inevitably strangle and suffocate, or at least blind, our vision of the prophet, the pastor and the priest in Everyman? *Abusus non tollit usum:* but the abuse of the sacred ministry and the holy place and the Sabbath, so that any expectation of finding the holy in the 'seven whole days', and on the shop floor at Vauxhall's, and in the boardroom, is negligible, has now a long and sad history. In our secular society there is also, of course, the question who should—and will—pay for the holy places, the historic churches and the cathedrals, and the large full-time ministry to be maintained. Or is the latter, as Bishop Lesslie Newbigin argues, a 'Constantinian' survival that must go? In our age of population explosion and the multi-racial city, often of more than a million, can there ever again be a priesthood to 'cover' society, as, for instance, the parochial system attempted to 'cover' Britain? And in a 'plural' society, in which people live in one place, learn in another, labour in another and spend their leisure in another, can the mystery man based only on where people live ever be anything but a shadow of the priesthood which was once at the hub of the one community in which people lived, learnt, laboured and spent their leisure? But who will 'hallow' the elemental events of life—marriage, birth, suffering, death—leave alone work and leisure (no! do *not* leave them alone!)? Who will help people to

7

perceive the mystery at the heart of their lives if there is not *some kind of priesthood*? Yet the provision of 'some kind of priesthood' is never simply the product of some kind of committee, but most often comes about because this man and that woman have felt called—and answered the call—to be 'stewards of the mysteries of God'. And to say this is in no way to despise the processes of recruitment, selection and training for 'stewards'. Many long hours of committee work have gone into the creation of, for instance, such schemes of theological education as the St Albans Ministerial Training Scheme. Sometimes these questions seem to have arrived on our doorsteps only in the last decades. At others they seem perennial problems, but thinly disguised, as old and older than the Jewish prophets. They have simply suddenly taken new and urgent forms. Certainly such questions are not for the Church of England alone—or even the Christian Church.

Martin Buber, the foremost Jewish thinker of our time—the centenary of his birth occurred this year—wrote in *Between Man and Man:*

In my earlier years the 'religious' was for me the exception. There were hours that were taken out of the course of things. From somewhere or other the firm crust of everyday was pierced. Then the reliable permanence of appearances broke down ... 'religious experience' was the experience of an otherness which did not fit into the context of life. It could begin with something customary, with consideration of some familiar object, but which then became unexpectedly mysterious and uncanny; finally lighting a way into the lightning-pierced darkness of the mystery itself ... the 'religious' lifted you out. Over there now lay the accustomed existence with its affairs, but here illumination and ecstasy and rapture held, without time or sequence.

The illegitimacy of such a division of the temporal life, which is streaming to death and eternity and which only in fulfilling its temporality can be fulfilled in face of these, was brought home to me by an everyday event. ... Since then I have given up the 'religious' which is nothing but the exception, extraction, exaltation, ecstasy; or it has given me up. I possess nothing but the everyday out of which I am never taken. The mystery is no longer disclosed, it has escaped or has made its dwelling here where everything happens as it happens.

Yes. That is what this book is about: the 'deep affinity between the mystery of God and the mystery of humanity'. It is not about some lack of knowledge which it could be that some branch of science may eventually fill; or about some unclear thinking which some philosopher may eventually make clear. Centrally, it is about the *Mystery of Being* itself. ('A mystery', said Gabriel Marcel, 'is something in which I am myself involved') And a black unemployed teenager in Brixton or Bedford has just as much and as desperate a need to know who he is as a top civil servant commuting from Radlett. Both alike are confronted by and involved in 'the Mystery'.

Patrick White sets an epigraph at the front of his novel *The Solid Mandala* which is an epigraph not only to all his work but also, I hope, to this volume:

There is another world,
    but it is in this one.

1. Ministry and Priesthood

Helen Oppenheimer

It is commonly answered that in arguments about priesthood, we can take ministry for granted. Ministry is supposed to be something we call fall back upon and talk about acceptably in terms of any doctrine of priesthood, high or low. Perhaps we want to assert that the special character of priesthood is such that only some (Levites, perhaps, or males, or the episcopally ordained) can be priests; but then we add that the others are not excluded from playing their part because there are many ministries. Or perhaps we look on priesthood as one particular kind of ministry which ought (or ought not) to be open to more of us. Or we may decide that we do not need priests, only ministers. Or, affirming Christ's unique priesthood, we can emphasize that all believers partake of it, though some exercise special ministries (thereby approximately reversing the first position). An Anglican may be more concerned to contain all these views within one Church than to decide between them, or may be chiefly anxious to affirm one or other of them as truth and act accordingly. But whether we want most to be Catholic or Protestant or comprehensive, the debate over priesthood seems enough to tackle: about ministry it seems quite sufficient to remember that it is service, not status. To raise difficulties about ministry too seems unnecessarily awkward; but sometimes the longest way round is the shortest way home.

The trouble is that ministry, much more than priesthood, is

11

what one might call a greedy concept. The notion of ministry tends to gobble up everything into itself so that it becomes impossible to sort out what is not ministry. All are ministers but some are more ministers than others. A priest is something definite, if only we could be sure of what. One either is or is not a priest, however difficult it proves to settle arguments about it. But with ministry, it is difficult to start the argument. 'They also serve who only stand and wait.' Who is anyone to say that someone else is not even standing and waiting? But then does it amount to much to call somebody a minister? Unless ministry can be distinguished from something else which is not ministry, it seems hardly worth talking about. But if we keep our distinction somewhere in the back of our minds without ever making it explicit, we may find ourselves guilty of a more subtle arrogance than the grandeur which besets the idea of priesthood.

Whatever priesthood is, ministry is service. 'We were put into the world to do good to others; but what were the others put here for?' a social worker is said to have wondered. The more the glory and satisfaction of loving service is preached, the less is left over for the 'others' to have any value in themselves. It was over sixty years ago that Saki pointed out bitterly that you can always tell them by their hunted expression. It is still worth being on the alert for the innocent unscrupulousness of the people who are determined to do good, even though we are far from having overcome the guilty unscrupulousness of the people who are determined to do evil and the inertia of the people who do not care which they do.

Of course there are several layers of human error and badness to be uncovered here, and the most obvious ones hide the ones underneath. God's courtiers, whether called priests or not, have not always been free of the vices and weaknesses of courtiers: time-serving, self-seeking and conceit. Even if spiritual privileges have not been claimed as crassly as earthly privileges, it has been hard not to presume that those closest to God professionally must be the most beloved by God.[1] So, trying to put this right, we say, and mean, 'service, not status',

1. Quick, *Essays in Orthodoxy*, p. 278

12

and endeavour to live up to this; and gradually and insensibly make service a new status which leaves those outside more beyond the pale than ever. What we need is Wordsworth's Old Cumberland Beggar to be the final recipient of our ministry.

> Scarcely do his feet
> Disturb the summer dust ...
> But deem not this Man useless.

He has a valuable and honourable role, for

> man is dear to man; the poorest poor
> Long for some moments in a weary life
> When they can know and feel that they have been,
> Themselves, the fathers and the dealers out
> Of some small blessings; have been kind to such
> As needed kindness, for this single cause
> That we have all of us one human heart.

The old man, whom 'even the slow-paced wagon leaves behind', is the ultimate type of the layman when everyone else is in one way or another a minister.

These reflections are occasioned by superimposing two unsolved problems of today upon one another. A woman could hardly write about Christian ministry now without being aware, perhaps primarily aware, of the question of ordaining women. For some, the answer is straightforward, one way or the other; but for many it is not straightforward, and what complicates it is uncertainty about what is being asked for and what is being refused. How can we say there is no theological objection to the ordination of women when we do not know who 'we' are when it comes to saying what 'we' understand ordination to mean? So the easiest if not the simplest answer comes up: wait. Yet for this answer to be either honest or practical, it needs to be filled out with some solid idea of what we are waiting for. So those of us who are becoming increasingly convinced that eventually women could be priests must press upon all our contemporaries the questions about priesthood and ministry which are still not only disputed but muddled. What is the grace of orders? Is it a privilege? What is a vocation and can women's vocations be as varied as men's?

But priesthood and ministry are already being scrutinized in a different context, conveniently called 'the auxiliary ministry' or the 'non-stipendiary ministry' to avoid the possibly tendentious 'worker priests' or 'part-time priests'. What sort of calling is it to serve God in a professional capacity? We cannot serve God and Mammon; but can we consecrate some to God's service while not taking them away from secular work? In what sense must vocation be full-time? What are we distinguishing the auxiliary ministry from? In fact, what is laity?

For the discussion is not just about how it becomes a servant of God to earn his living. (He can make tents, but can he make beer?) It is about what constitutes a servant of God. Sooner or later this question too must take the form, What is the point of ordination? There has been much emphasis lately on what the laity, the non-ordained, can and should do. They can administer church finances, witness for their faith, visit the sick, comfort the bereaved, study theology, teach and even preach, lead prayers, baptize in theory though seemingly not in practice. They cannot by definition perform the priestly functions of consecration and absolution; but surely we do not want people ordained merely as 'massing priests' to say certain words? Surely there is something between superstitious ritualism on the one hand and mere commissioning on the other which in some way sets a person apart? But in what way?

The question is not only, What cannot the non-ordained, the laity, do? but, In what capacity are they doing all the things they can do? Is baptism a kind of ordination? Are lay people the real 'worker priests'? When we say politely that we must regain understanding of the ministry of the laity, are we not really asking once again, What is the ministry of the ones left over from whatever ministry we were talking about? Or, even more bluntly, What is lacking in being lay? The question readily takes this form for somebody who has never been offered the choice whether to be lay or not. So the problem of

14

auxiliary ministry can arouse more awkwardly feminist feelings than the direct question about whether or not to support
the ordination of women forthwith.

But perhaps after all this so-to-speak *rag-bag theory of laity* is
a logical mistake. Perhaps laity is not a basket into which we
put whatever is left over when we have sorted out all the more
definite kinds of ministry. If it were, no wonder we have
nothing very constructive to say about the role of lay people as
such. It is excellent to be an Old Cumberland Beggar if one is
already filling that role, but much less satisfactory to expect
someone to adopt it. Do we have to look for a role for lay
people at all? Ministry is a role and it is wrong to make it a
status: but that does not mean that there is no such thing as
status. Let us try out the supposition that laity is a status and
that it is a mistake to make it a role. Then perhaps we can
hope to talk sense about who can fill what role.

To explain this suggestion, we can revive a distinction of St
Augustine's and say that ministry is something to be *used*,
whereas laity is not just something to be used in a different
way but is meant to be *enjoyed*. Or, more simply, we can com-
pare ministry to a funnel. A Christian minister is someone
through whom God's grace and goodness are given; but God's
grace and goodness do not travel on *through* for ever: they come
to rest somewhere, and where but upon God's people, His
laity? If ministry is characteristically a 'through' concept, then
laity is something quite different, a 'stop' concept, an end
rather than a means. The Christian ministry can easily seem
like the children's game of 'pass the parcel', in which the one
found holding the parcel when the music stops is out. It ought
to be more like a postal service trying to deliver parcels to their
right destinations; and presumably postmen also hope to
receive mail themselves. Whatever it means to affirm the
priesthood of all believers, it would be well to affirm also the
laity of all priests. Ordained or not, we are to be God's people,
not only his ministers, recipients, not only channels, of his
love. Baptism, whereby we become God's people, is not a
commissioning to a role but an entry upon a heritage. To call
laity a status may sound presumptuous; but of course it is a
status given, not a status earned as of right. To feed at God's

15

table should be quite as awe-inspiring as to wait at it. The royal invitation 'Friend, come up higher' is not a summons to be taken lightly. The holy has always been the terrible, and no less so when if offers us privileges out of relation to our deserving. The consciousness of lay status as a gift need be no more corruptible than the consciousness of ministerial role as a vocation. It is when status and role are muddled that, uncertain where we stand, we scramble into competitiveness and arrogance.

A different way of saying all this is to say that if ministers are 'stewards of the mysteries of God', their stewardship is on behalf of someone. The concept of stewardship is dependent upon the concept of *ownership*. God is the rightful Owner; but the whole point of the Christian faith is that God shares what He owns. God's people are his adopted children, 'and if children, then heirs, heirs of God and fellow heirs with Christ',[2] immature maybe but heirs as distinct from slaves.

Our status as adopted children of God is for us to enter into and enjoy. There is nothing wrong, quite the contrary, with taking this 'enjoy' in its fullest human meaning. 'Is it not a Great Thing', said Thomas Traherne, 'that you should be Heir of the World? Is it not a very Enriching Veritie?'[3] So he went on to celebrate this status of ours. 'You never Enjoy the World aright, till the Sea it self floweth in your Veins, till you are Clothed with the Heavens, and Crowned with the Stars: and Perceiv your self to be the Sole Heir of the whole World: and more then so, becaus Men are in it who are every one Sole Heirs, as well as you.'[4] Christian ministry ought to be a means to this enjoyment of the people of God, and Christian ministers ought to be stewards of this mystery.

If we can gain the kind of understanding of our *status* as God's people which makes mystery more vivid, we can inquire less fretfully into the variegated *roles* which are the forms of service that make mystery accessible. To have something to say which is neither presumption nor moonshine, we must

2. [a]Rom. 8:15–17. Cf. Gal.
3. *Centuries of Meditation, 3*
4. ibid., 29

stress both the awesomeness and the availability of the mystery. Traherne knew very well that our heritage which exalted him so depends upon the hard earthly fact of the Cross,[5] which gives no scope for arrogance or vagueness. The point of the Christian mystery is that it takes bodily form. It is sacramental.

The continuing pledge of this awesomeness and availability is the Eucharist, given to God's people through particular human agents. To think on these lines can suggest a high but not superstitious understanding of the role of those ministers whose stewardship is eucharistic. Whatever we believe about sacrificial priesthood, we can say that Christian priests are at least God's major-domos. They are entrusted with the task of welcoming God's people into His presence ('Real Presence', we may well say) and offering them his hospitality and sustenance in tangible form. So in asking who can exercise this ministry for us all,[6] we are asking who is capable of filling this role.

In other words, the Christian sacraments make God's holiness findable. So an individual person, however pleasing and however eligible to God, who for good reasons or bad cannot make the mysteries of God tangible to God's people, cannot exercise a fully valid ministry. This is how it can be a proper theological decision to wait, even to wait a long while, to make changes which could destroy or delay the unity of the Church. Though the duty to wait for what one thinks eventually right is not absolute, for it can become a cover for procrastination or scrupulosity, it ought not to be called a matter of 'mere expediency'. Nor does 'wait' mean 'reject'. What it calls for is a more generous and profound attempt to pursue the discussion.

To remind one another now that ministry is much wider than priesthood and that the Eucharist is not the only means of grace can look like a too soothing way of stopping the argument. On the contrary, it needs to be said as a way of widening it. The Christian faith is sacramental through and through, and the mysteries of God take many bodily forms.

5. ibid., 88.9ff.
6. Cf. Quick, *Essays in Orthodoxy*, p. 283

Wherever the holy is made available for us, those who handle holy things on our behalf must be mindful of the awesomeness of the mystery, and need consecration for the task. To study theology, to teach, to preach, to counsel, to comfort, to administer, to intercede are all ways of taking more upon ourselves than we can humanly manage. To presume to do these things in one's own strength is sacrilege. It is not superstitious to consider that God's holiness could be dangerous to the careless in the way that an electric current is dangerous; though 'earthing' is a happier application of the metaphor than 'insulation'. To allow people to minister in God's Church without giving proper thought to the sorts of blessing they need is to trifle with the mystery.

It may be that a significant part of the discontent of those whose Christian ministry has to be outside the priesthood is not their inability to celebrate the Eucharist but the feeling that their ministry is inadequately supported. This is a matter not of rights but of needs. To enter a profession is normally to be incorporated in a body, in which one's individual fragility, one-sidedness, gaucheness or overweeningness can be contained. Surely a great deal of what is experienced as 'the grace of orders' is mediated through this aspect of professional belonging. It is something like this that people mean by the inaccurate but not meaningless expression, 'He has gone into the Church'. Neither solemn commissioning of an *individual* nor talk about the blessed company of *all* faithful people can be a complete substitute for the upholding of a Christian minister (male or female, stipendiary or non-stipendiary) by the particular support of a body of *colleagues*. Heaven forbid that we should play down the priestly role of presiding at the Eucharist for the sake of those who are not eligible to exercise it; but there is a great deal of scope for enlarging our understanding of the sacramental character of all Christian ministry and of the diverse ways in which people can make the mysteries of God accessible to one another.

All this is about roles and the strengthening of people to fill them for us, so that they can be vehicles of God's grace for us all. The object of the whole exercise is not the vehicles but the destination, and the destination is that God shall be present

18

with his people. To travel hopefully is not better than to arrive: rather, 'There remaineth yet a sabbath rest for the people of God', when ministry is swallowed up in fulfilment like faith and hope in love. If we shift the metaphor a little and look on the Churches as the vehicles, we can think of ourselves, not too seriously, as parties setting off for holidays at the seaside. Sometimes we can take turns with the driving; often we crawl in traffic jams; we play games to amuse the children; maybe we get lost; maybe the journey is itself enjoyable; but at the end of it drivers and passengers together hope to arrive at the magical place where we suddenly smell the sea and find it as the promised horizon to our road.

2. The Pauline Background

Geoffrey Lampe

'The apostolic ministry' has become a tedious catch-phrase in modern ecumenical diplomacy. Identified with 'the historic episcopate', the apostolic ministry is something which Churches may possess (sometimes through the accidents of sixteenth-century politics), receive from others, or take into their various systems. Apostolic ministry as the Apostle himself understood it belongs to a different world of ideas altogether. Paul does not use the actual phrase; but his conception of the ministry proper to apostles is succinctly described by him in his first letter to the Corinthians: 'So let a man take account of us as of Christ's servants, and stewards of the mysteries of God' (1 Cor.4:1).

Most of Paul's reflections about his own vocation to apostleship and how he fulfilled it in his ministry of evangelism and of service to his churches were forced out of him by the pressure of opposition. It was because his Corinthian converts had split into factions, each of which had developed a personality cult of a particular leader either of the local mission or of the Christian movement in general, Paul himself, Apollos and Cephas (possibly also with the ultimate in spiritual one-upmanship, a self-styled 'Christ party'), that he found himself forced to explain and defend the nature of the ministry which he and his fellow apostles were carrying out (1 Cor.1:12). When he asks that 'a man should reckon us to be Christ's servants' he means by 'us', at any rate in the first instance, Apollos and himself

21

(3:4,4:6). Paul was himself the founder of the church in Corinth: 'I planted'. Apollos had evidently come in at a later stage as a reinforcement to the mission, as Luke also indicates in Acts 18:27—19:1: 'Apollos watered', says Paul. What Paul, however, insists on, against any kind of charismatic leadership, in the false modern sense of 'charisma', is that 'neither he who plants nor he who waters is anything'; all that is important in this situation is not any human leadership, but God who produces the crop (3:6–7). Apollos and Paul are no more than servants or ministers (*diaconoi*) through whom the Corinthians had been converted; and even the making of a convert, the bringing of a person to Christian belief, is not something which lies within the power of the minister to bring about: faith is evoked not by the human instrument, but 'according as God gives to each person' (3:5).

This, then, is the apostolic ministry. It is a servant's ministry in which the apostle counts for nothing except in so far as he is used by God as a channel of communication; and the nature of divine communication to man implies that the apostolic ministry is essentially a prophetic ministry. It is, perhaps, somewhat strange to reflect that if Paul could return to take part in our modern controversies about church order, and heard it said that some particular church lacked the fullness of the apostolic ministry, he would probably conclude that it must somehow be without preachers and teachers. For the apostleship which he himself exercised involved being an *hyperetes Christou*, a servant or assistant of Christ. This is a term which recalls Luke's description of the earliest witnesses and handers-on of the tradition of the gospel events: *hyperetai tou logou*, ministers of the word (Luke 1:2), a description which Luke later applies to Paul himself when describing the commission which he received on the Damascus road, to be 'a minister and a witness both of those things which you have seen, and of those things in which I will appear to you' (Acts 26:16). It is as communicators of the Lord's word that the apostles are ministers of Christ.

It is in this same sense that they are stewards (*oikonomoi*) of God's mysteries. They are servants, indeed, but trusted servants like the faithful steward of Luke 12:42, dispensers of the

22

provision made by their master for his people. This does not, of course, mean that Paul regarded the apostles as administrators in the sense of ecclesiastical bureaucrats. As Professor Kingsley Barrett remarks in his commentary on 1 Corinthians, 'The chapter as a whole (see especially iv.9–13) makes it impossible to think of the apostolate as an ecclesiastical civil service.' What the apostle 'dispenses' is God's word or self-communication to his human creation. His task is like that of the Hebrew prophet, permitted by God to listen to his own counsels and to declare them to his people. It is also like that of the Greek philosopher-preacher; commentators on this passage have often called attention to Epictetus' description of the Cynic preacher as a minister (*hyperetes*) of Zeus and as a steward (*oikonomos*). The apostle is one who dispenses the mysteries of God. 'Mystery' in this context is virtually synonymous with 'revelation'. Apostolic ministry is a ministry which enables men to receive what God wills to disclose to them; it is a channel for the communication of a revealed reality.

'Mystery', in the sense in which Paul uses the term, does not bear the meanings to which it has generally been reduced in modern English. A 'mystery' is not a puzzle, like the plot of a mystery story or detective novel, nor could Paul or any other New Testament writer speak of something secret or unexplained being 'wrapped in mystery'. On the contrary, if his mysteries are secrets they are, somewhat paradoxically, open secrets. They are not mysterious in the sense of being concealed; rather, they are disclosures. What differentiates them from the truths that are the ordinary objects of our everyday understanding is that they are not apprehended by human cleverness, Paul's 'wisdom of this age' (1 Cor. 2:6), but revealed by the Spirit of God (2:10–16). Mysteries are God's own counsels, his providential dispositions for his creatures and especially his eschatological purposes for man's salvation. They lie beyond the scope of our unaided reason and imagination, and in this sense they are secret, belonging to 'the hidden wisdom of God' (2:7); or rather, they would be secret and hidden had not God chosen to disclose them in the gospel of which the apostles are the missionary 'stewards'.

The verbs associated by the New Testament writers with

the noun 'mystery' are not those which indicate either the keeping of a secret or the solution of a problem by a process of investigation. They are the words for disclosure, communication and publication. In Pauline language what one does to a mystery is to 'proclaim' it, 'tell' it, 'speak of' it, 'make' it 'plain' (Col. 1:28,1 Cor. 2:1 reading *mysterion*; 1 Cor. 15:51,1 Cor. 2:7,14:2, Col. 4:3, Rom. 16:25–26, Col. 1:26, 4:4). The seer of the Apocalypse characteristically 'sees' a mystery (Rev.1:20). The mysteriousness of a mystery is not its hiddenness but its transcendence. It is given to us from a source that lies beyond our own selves in the eternal divine wisdom, and it is apprehended through the unpredictable and uncontrollable inspiration of the Spirit of God in the human heart and mind. It is not mysterious in the sense that it is not to be made public or that it is not meant to be generally understood.

A glance at those passages of the New Testament where the word 'mystery' occurs will indicate something of the content of this divine disclosure. According to Mark (4:11), reproduced by the other Synoptists, 'the mysteries of the Kingdom of God' were revealed directly to the inner circle of chosen disciples and not, as to others, through parables. These disciples resemble Moses, or the authentic prophets who are 'like Moses' (Deut.34:10,18:15,18); with them God speaks 'mouth to mouth and not in dark sayings' (Num.12:8). What is communicated to them is God's purpose for the salvation of men by bringing them into his kingdom, with the implication that in some sense the ministry of Jesus is the present anticipation of that eschatological goal. In the Pauline letters, which, especially if Ephesians is reckoned among them, contain many more instances of the use of 'mystery' than the other New Testament writings, it may stand for some particular aspect of God's revealed purpose. In Romans 11:25 it is the paradoxical dispensation of providence by which Israel's present blindness to the gospel is to lead to the conversion of the Gentiles and this, in turn, to the ultimate salvation of all Israel. In 1 Corinthians 15:51 it is the revelation of the future transformation which is to make it possible for what is mortal to put on immortality and what is corruptible to put on incorruptibility, even though material flesh and blood cannot inherit the King-

24

dom of God. In the letter to the Ephesians the mystery is God's revealed purpose of bringing the Gentiles within the scope of salvation and uniting them with the Jews in a universal unity in Christ (1:9,3:3,9). The thought of this particular revelation leads the author on to speak of the mystery in more general terms as 'the mystery of Christ' (3:4), or 'the mystery of the gospel' (6:19): that is to say, the revelation of salvation for all men in and through Christ, which is the basic content of the apostles' message. This general sense, in which mystery is synonymous with the gospel, the word of God, and with Christ himself as the revelation of God, is very characteristic of Paul's thought. In Romans 16:25–26, a passage reminiscent of the letter to the Ephesians and unlikely to be an authentic part of Romans, the words 'revelation' and 'mystery' are brought together; the revelation of the mystery is virtually equated with the 'gospel' and with the 'preaching' (*kerygma*) of Jesus Christ. Its content is Christ himself; this is the mystery which was kept in silence through the ages but which has now been disclosed through the writings of the prophets.

It is worth noticing here what Paul's answer seems to be to the question *how* the Spirit communicates the revelation to us. It is not simply through flashes of inspired insight. In part, at least, it is through the prophetic writings, that is, through the Scriptures. This is in line with the claim made in the letter to the Ephesians that the mystery of Christ has not been made known to men in past generations, but that it is now revealed to 'his holy apostles and prophets' in, or by, the Spirit (3:5). This phrase, which may well be an indication of post-Pauline and sub-apostolic authorship, signifies that God's revelation has been communicated either through the preaching of the apostles and Christian prophets, that is to say, through the tradition which came to be embodied in the New Testament, or, if, as may possibly be the case, 'prophets' refers here to the Hebrew prophets, through a combination of the Old Testament prophecies and the apostolic witness to their fulfilment in Christ. In the latter case the writer is saying that the mystery has been revealed to the Old Testament prophets 'now'. This, paradoxical as it may seem, is not impossible. It would mean that it is only now, in the light of the Christ-event, that

25

the true meaning of the Old Testament Scriptures has been disclosed. It is as though even their authors, the ancient prophets, have only now been enabled to understand the true significance of what they themselves were saying long ago.

Paul himself believed that the hidden counsel of God is revealed to spiritually mature Christians by God's Spirit; this means no less than that 'we have the mind of Christ' (1 Cor.2:10,16). It is, however, in his view, largely through the Scriptures that the Spirit communicates this revelation. He reads it out of the Old Testament, as his constant appeal to the scriptural text makes clear. On the other hand, his interpretation of what the 'prophetic writings' said is highly original and often idiosyncratic. If the Spirit uses the Old Testament to speak to Paul about the mystery of Christ, this happens because in the light of what he believes already about Christ Paul re-reads the Old Testament with fresh eyes. Christ is read into the Scriptures and then, again, read out of them. It seems, therefore, that there is less contrast than there might appear to be at first sight between revelation through flashes of inspired insight and revelation through Scripture. Scripture, it would seem, serves both to trigger off, as it were, Paul's own highly original understanding of the gospel and also to legitimate it and provide it with authoritative confirmation; but in either case it is Scripture as reinterpreted by himself. For Paul the appeal to Scripture is thus, as it always must be, a somewhat circular process.

Other Pauline passages illustrate the use of 'mystery' in the general sense of the divine plan of salvation through Christ (1 Cor.2:7) or, simply, the content of the Christian proclamation, as in 1 Corinthians 2:1, where Paul reminds his readers how he came to Corinth proclaiming 'the mystery of God' or, according to a strongly supported variant reading, 'the testimony of God', that is, the preacher's witness to the act of God in Christ. In 1 Corinthians 13:2 to 'know all mysteries' is to possess the gift of prophetic inspiration in the highest possible degree, and so to 'stand in God's counsel' (cf.Jer.23:22) and know his purpose. Paul tells the Colossians (1:25–26) of the stewardship (*oikonomia*) entrusted to him by God, which is to carry out the full preaching of God's word; and the word of

God is identified with the mystery or revelation which is Christ himself, present among the Gentiles. So, again, the word which Paul preaches is the mystery of Christ (4:3) and Christ is himself the content of God's revelation (*mysterion*, 2:2).

Occasionally in the New Testament 'mystery' denotes some particular mode of divine disclosure: the new meaning, or real meaning, of a text of Scripture when read afresh in the light of the Christ-event, such as the reinterpretation of Genesis 2:24 as a prophecy of the marriage of Christ and his Church (Eph.5:32), the significance of objects seen in a vision (Rev.1:20), or the symbolism of a name or code-word, like 'Babylon' in Revelation 17:5 (though in Revelation 10:7 'mystery' retains its wider sense and stands for the divine purpose in history, revealed to the prophets). In the patristic writings it very often denotes the inner meaning or revelatory significance of a sacramental sign or rite, so that *mysterion* comes actually to mean 'sacrament', but there is no sacramental connotation in the New Testament usage of the term.

In two Pauline passages the sense is somewhat less clear. 'A person who speaks in a "tongue" does not speak to men but to God. For no one hears, but in the Spirit he speaks mysteries' (1 Cor.14:12). This probably does not mean that he speaks mysteriously in the modern sense of saying things that cannot be understood. More probably, he is actually uttering revelations, that is, prophecies, but no one can hear him since his words are unintelligible. It might, perhaps, even be translated, 'For no one hears, even though in the Spirit he speaks of God's counsel.' 'The mystery of lawlessness', it says in 2 Thessalonians 2:7, 'is already operating.' This, again, would seem to mean that the crescendo of apostasy which is to precede the End, an apostasy conceived on the model of the events of the Maccabaean times, is itself a part of the divine plan, and as such it forms part of the content of revelation.

Characteristically, it is in the Pastoral Epistles that the meaning of 'mystery', like so many other aspects of the Pauline gospel, seems to be transposed into another key, at once defensive and institutionalized. 'The mystery of the faith' is now something to be 'kept' or 'held' by the deacons of the

Church (1 Tim.3:9), and 'the mystery of piety' can be encapsulated in a credal hymn (3:16). Revelation is coming to be equated with doctrinal formulations; faith is passing over into 'the Faith', a system of belief rather than personal trust in God through Christ. From this point it is no long step to the concept of 'the Faith once for all delivered to the saints' of Jude 3.

This raises the profoundly difficult question of the relation between revelation on the one hand and doctrine on the other. What in fact is the content of that given and transcendent mystery? What is it that those apostolic stewards actually dispense? Certainly, their task cannot be to dole out revealed truths, for revelation is not given in the form of propositions dictated from heaven, and all our statements of belief, our theological and ethical formulations, are not timeless and irreformable truths but tentative, provisional, incomplete and culturally conditioned attempts to interpret, and to draw inferences from, revelatory experience. At every point and at all times they are subject to the relativities of history. Divine revelation itself is always mediated in and through the finite and fallible reason and emotions of human beings. Scripture is no exception. Not only is Scripture liable to be interpreted differently by almost every reader in the light of his own presuppositions and those of the society to which he belongs, but in itself it does no more than record the experience of human beings who believed that they had been addressed by God and that God had disclosed himself to them—a conviction shared equally by those whose experience forms the subject-matter of the sacred books of other religions. Nowhere is there any absolutely authoritative body of truth to be dispensed to the faithful for their unquestioning acceptance.

Yet in and through the experience of human beings the Spirit of God does communicate revelation: an awareness of the transcendent supervening upon the normalities of day-to-day existence, mediated in many different modes, always almost beyond the power of human thought to analyse and the ability of human language to describe. It is a personal revelation, the coming to a man of an awareness of a relationship or, rather, of a conviction that he has actually received the possibility of a relationship, to which the language of 'grace' or

28

gracious unmerited love, moral demands, and, 'calling' is appropriate—a relationship which presents itself concretely in the picture drawn by the Evangelists of the life and death of Jesus, and which expresses itself in terms of 'Christlike' living, characterized by the Pauline 'fruit of the Spirit' and the unselfseeking, God-like love portrayed in 1 Corinthians 13. Such an awareness of relationship cannot be pinned down in theological and ethical formulations, though these may help to illustrate it. It has always to be explored—explored, indeed, into infinity, always to be reinterpreted, always to be freshly understood in the realization that every attempt to understand it is no more than provisional and is liable to be superseded. Yet it is communicable, more easily in practice than in teaching or preaching. It seems that the mystery is more readily 'dispensed' through the communal sharing of the basic experience of that dimly understood transcendent relationship.

If this is so, the answer to the question, 'What is this mystery?' appears to be closely bound up with the question, 'Who are its stewards?' The myth of a transmission of an articulated system of belief, a 'deposit' of divinely revealed truths, in orderly sequence from Jesus to the Twelve Apostles, to the duly ordained ministry of the Catholic Church (the myth, in fact, of an 'apostolic age', developed by Luke and the author of the Pastoral Epistles and systematized in the second century), can claim no support from Paul. His own credentials as a legitimate apostle seemed to some to be highly dubious. The status of Apollos as a missionary seems to have presented a puzzle to Luke; certainly Luke's account of him has puzzled every commentator on Acts. Apollos had been catechized in the (Christian) way of the Lord (where and by whom?), he was fervent in the Spirit and taught accurately the things concerning Jesus, yet he 'knew only John's baptism'. But when, a few lines further on, Paul meets 'disciples' (possibly converts of Apollos?) who had been baptized only into John's baptism, he finds them apparently unaware that John had told those whom he baptized to believe in the one who was to come after him, Jesus, and unaware, too, that 'there is Holy Spirit'. Furthermore, Paul proceeds to baptize them in the name of the Lord Jesus. Yet Apollos was merely taken by

29

Priscilla and Aquila, Paul's missionary colleagues, and given a 'more accurate' exposition of the way of God (Acts 18:24–26,19:2–7). Luke is clearly at pains to present Apollos in the best possible light; but he evidently realizes that Apollos, who suddenly enters the scene out of nowhere, needed to be 'regularized' in some way before he could be regarded, from Luke's point of view, as an authentic partner in the Pauline mission. Where Apollos' original commission came from Paul does not tell us, and Luke obviously has no idea. Paul's own authority as an apostle depended entirely, in the last resort, on his own personal belief that, in a private visionary experience like that of Isaiah and other Old Testament prophets, God had 'revealed his Son' to him (Gal.1:16) in order that he should preach the good news of him to the Gentiles. That this 'call' was genuine was acknowledged by others, including the 'pillar' apostles of the Jerusalem church. But the only criterion to distinguish a true prophet from a false, an authentic vocation from self-delusion, is the test 'By their fruits. . . .'; and what mattered to Paul by way of confirmation that he really had received an apostleship 'not from men nor through man, but through Christ and God who raised him from the dead' (Gal.1:1), was the tangible evidence of the results of his work. It had been attested by the 'signs and wonders and mighty acts' which are the signs of an apostle (2 Cor.12:12), and his converts are 'the seal of his apostleship' (1 Cor.9:2).

Stewardship of the mysteries of God is certainly not restricted, then, to an 'ordained ministry'. Apostolic ministry, as Paul describes it, is a prophetic ministry, and in the Christian Church no one is ordained as a prophet; all that the community can do with a person who speaks and acts as a prophet is to test him by his 'fruits' and recognize him as one who has been called and sent by God. According to Paul, the first and most important of these 'fruits' is Christlikeness; and this is easily recognizable, for it involves a most literal and stark following of Christ along the way of the Cross:

I think that God has set forth us the apostles last of all, like men condemned to death . . . a gazing-stock to the world,

30

to angels and to men. We are fools for Christ's sake, we are weak, dishonoured, we are hungry and thirsty and naked and beaten up, without fixed abode, toiling, insulted, persecuted, slandered; we are made as the filth of the world (as the King James Version has it) and are the offscouring of all things unto this day.

In the last resort, it seems that only an apostolic ministry which can show some of these marks of recognition can really 'dispense' revelations.

3. Love's Recognition

W. H. Vanstone

Peter, in his early twenties, went to spend a week-end at his fiancée's, and on the Sunday morning they attended early Communion at the local church—a dual-purpose building recently opened on a housing estate. Peter told me afterwards about the church.

It looked quite nice from the outside, and the inside wasn't bad either, except that the floor was a real mess. There was litter—toffee papers, cigarette ends, that kind of thing—all over it. However, before the service started the vicar explained. He said that they have to use the Church for parties and things as well as services, and though they usually get it all cleaned up for Sunday, on that particular Saturday night they had finished very late and hadn't got around to cleaning up. So the vicar said he wanted to apologize to us. Well, it was good of him to explain and apologize, but, dash it all, he shouldn't have apologized to us: he should have apologized to God.

I have often thought about this remark. Priggish? Possibly: but not, I think, if one knew the speaker. Naïve? Primitive? Possibly again: but if so, not characteristic of the speaker. I think it might be a rather profound remark.

Peter's indignation seems to imply that in the way the church is, something important is at stake, and that what is at

33

stake is something other than the state of mind of people. The vicar's apology to the congregation may well have removed any sense of an affront to themselves; they may well have understood and been able to worship that morning in perfect charity towards the organizers of the party and the vicar and everyone else. The state of mind of the congregation may have been as satisfactory on that morning as on any other morning; the presence of the litter, once the apology had been made, may have made no difference at all. To all the people present the litter may no longer have mattered. Nevertheless, Peter seems to imply, it may still have mattered to God.

Yes, perhaps Peter was naïve: perhaps his idea of God was primitive—the idea of a deity who looks for tokens and gestures of respect and is affronted when he does not receive them. The idea of a God who is possessive and demanding in quite trivial ways is not unknown in the history of religion. Perhaps Peter had not heard of the God who requires mercy and not sacrifice, a certain state of mind in his people and not clean church floors. Perhaps it *was* a primitive sort of remark; but let us give it the benefit of the doubt and consider a little further what it implies.

It clearly implies, in the first place, that the way the world is *matters* to God. Peter does not seem to believe, as some people do, that since God's will and purpose must prevail *in any case,* nothing that exists or happens in the world can have any bearing on the fulfilment of his will and purpose. It is certainly reassuring to believe that nothing in the world can frustrate the purpose of God; but this belief undoubtedly carries the implication that nothing in the world ultimately matters. It implies that nothing is really *at stake* in the way the world is. It implies that nothing in the world has ultimate meaning, that nothing means anything to God. If God's will must prevail in any case, then anything in the world is dispensable: there is nothing upon which God must depend or wait for the fulfilment of his purpose.

Perhaps this is in fact the case, but if it is it becomes exceedingly difficult to believe that the relationship of God to the world is a relationship of love. For to love something is to make it matter to oneself; to give it the power to mean some-

34

thing to oneself; to make oneself dependent, for the issue of one's loving, upon the response or receiving of that other which one loves. Everyone who loves is aware of surrendering his detachment, his independence, of making himself vulnerable in a way in which he was not vulnerable before. So if the relationship of God to the world is a relationship of love, then God must wait upon the world for its response: become exposed in and to the world which he loves: become dependent on the way the world is for the fulfilment—or frustration—of his own loving endeavour. If God loves the world, then he gives to it the power to matter to himself, the power to make a difference to himself. He gives it power of meaning as well as power of being. Perhaps something of this was in Peter's mind when he suggested that there should have been an apology *to God* for the litter.

Peter's remark also implies, quite clearly, that the way the world is materially and physically matters to God: that *things* matter as well as states of mind and intentions and feelings. Now of course Jesus had to remind his contemporaries that the 'inside' of the world matters—the clean thoughts of men, the purity of the heart. But he did not deny that the 'outside' matters too. He did not suggest that the human heart 'being in the right place' is *all* that matters. Jesus certainly implied that sparrows matter to God; and, though it is unfair to take out of context St Paul's remark apropos of the text 'Thou shalt not muzzle the ox when it treadeth out the corn'—namely, 'God is not concerned with cattle'—Jesus could hardly have agreed with that remark as it stands.

Presumably the people who left litter on the floor did not *mean* any disrespect to God. Their state of mind was not irreverent, their intentions were entirely proper, and perhaps it was better that with good intentions they should have left the floor unswept than that they should have swept it in abject fear or in self-righteous satisfaction at their own diligence. But Peter seems to believe that the actual state of a floor matters to God as well as the intentions of those who do or do not sweep it. In this he is perhaps representative of his generation. For one seems to observe more often in the rising generation than in their elders a sense that the world, the physical, material,

35

non-human world, has *a worth of its own*: a worth which is not reducible, even in the last analysis, to its worth to man. One observes among the younger generation an increasing sense that the natural world matters *for its own sake*—whether or not it conduces to man's material well-being or his aesthetic satisfaction or his spiritual edification. One has heard it said by a young person that 'humanism is beginning to seem rather parochial': he implied that what matters in the world is not limited to what is happening, or will happen in the long run, to or within the human race. There is a growing belief that the survival of a species or a habitat matters even if, for the sake of its survival, man must be excluded from any kind of contact with it or investigation of it. There is a growing sense of a worth in creatures and things which is not limited to the support or pleasure or edification which they may provide, now or in the future, to mankind.

This belief does not always—or often—express itself in explicitly religious terms, and it certainly raises many problems. But, although it is observed most frequently in the younger generation, it does not seem to be simply naïve. It surely accords more easily with the biblical doctrine of creation than do those attitudes which imply that nothing in the world ultimately matters save the state of human consciousness: the God of the Bible would not feel particularly at home in Bloomsbury. Perhaps Peter was expressing a deep understanding of that doctrine in suggesting that a littered floor may be a blot or scar on the creation even when it gives no offence to human sensitivity, even if it is unobserved by any human eye.

The litter was on the floor of a church. Peter did not explicitly say that the vicar should have apologized to God for the litter being *there*, in that particular place; but he probably meant this. He probably felt that litter in a church mattered more than litter in a neighbouring field or lay-by. Was he naïve in this—in supposing that the way the church is matters more to God than the way the world in general is? Certainly there is an attitude which attributes to God a certain proprietory or partisan interest in the church; and certainly this attitude can degrade and trivialize the very concept of God. A

36

God who is only interested in the church, a God obsessed by what is happening in the church, is scarcely worth believing in. But Peter is not necessarily expressing this attitude. He is not implying that nothing is at stake in the condition of a field or lay-by, provided that no human eye is going to see it: he is only implying that more is at stake in the condition of a church.

There is reason to believe that he is right. For the church seems to have little reason for existing except as the 'place' (or the 'activity' or the 'community') where the activity of God, and the nature of that activity, is *recognized*. The loving activity of God is *happening* in fields and lay-bys and in all the world: in all the world God is exposed to the triumph or tragedy of his loving endeavour: to all the world, because he created it in love, God gives power of meaning. But it is also the case— unless the Christian religion is altogether erroneous—not only that God has offered to the world the possibility of receiving (or failing to receive) his loving creativity, but also that he has offered, at least to that fragment of the world which is man- kind, the greater possibility of recognizing the nature of that creativity. We say 'the *greater* possibility'; for, since love is a limitless self-giving, every particular gift or act of love can be only a sign or symbol of a yet larger generosity, a yet more generous will to do or give; and this larger generosity can be received only when the particular act or gift is *recognized* as a sign of love. So God, for the sake of that which he loves, has made his love *recognizable;* he has *declared* or *disclosed* his love. The *raison d'être* of the Church is to respond not simply to the activity of divine love (for every fragment of the world may so respond) but also to the *disclosure* of that love. Therefore it is the peculiar function of the Church to recognize what, at the deepest level, is happening in the world, to recognize what is actually at stake in the way the world is; and this recognition is to be a response—not merely a passive awareness but a freely chosen, responsive activity. When the Church fails to recognize what is at stake in that which immediately confronts it, in that which it has immediate power to remedy, in the litter on its own floor, then there is, one might say, a blot on the Church as well as a scar on the creation. If it matters to

37

God when his creation is scarred, then surely it must matter in a further sense when his Church fails to recognize that it matters. Perhaps Peter understood this. He certainly thought that the litter mattered to God; perhaps he also thought that it mattered to God that the vicar did not recognize that it mattered.

The *raison d'être*, the responsibility, of the Church is to recognize what is happening in the world, and what is actually at stake in what is happening. What is at stake is the triumph or the tragedy of the love of God. Recognizing the sublimity of what is at stake, the Church will strive that certain things rather than certain other things should happen, and in this striving will often make common cause with other agencies with different motivation. But the unique and distinctive responsibility of the Church is to express and preserve and proclaim its *recognition* of what is at stake.

This is the 'mystery of god' of which we are the appointed stewards. We are not the stewards of God's particular will and purpose, possessed of private information about 'what God wants' in Rhodesia or in the field of education or in the planning departments of Town Halls or even in the decisions of individual people. We only know that, if God is love, he wants 'what is best' for his beloved world; and what is in fact best in a particular case we can judge only by using those tools of reason and common sense and experience and reflection which are available in greater or lesser degree to all men. Nor are we stewards of God's grace and favour, dispensing it according to certain rules or by certain procedures. One might say that God needs no stewards or other intermediaries to reveal his will or bestow his grace. God *needs* only that which love itself needs—the response of the beloved other, without which love's own work of giving remains incomplete. God needs the receiving of the world in order that he may give to it all the richness of being; God needs the recognition of the Church in order that he may give to the world the yet greater richness of love itself. Love itself can be given only when its particular gifts are recognized as tokens of love—only, so to speak, when someone perceives and reads the small label which is attached unobtrusively to the gift. Love does not compel its own recognition, for that would be a kind of blackmail; but it makes it possible—for only so can its own self-giving become completed. The Church, one might say, *is* that possibility. It depends upon the Church whether or not there shall be recognized in the world the depth of love which is expended in and for the world's own being; and there is no greater tragedy than that where love is given it should pass unrecognized.

4. By Way of Blackpool Tower

Richard Holloway

She now lives in the geriatric ward of a general hospital, but
for years I brought the Holy Communion to her at home. She
lived up a dark Edinburgh tenement. I finally had to get a key
to her tiny flat, because she fell once trying to let me in and lay
in the hall for fifteen minutes before she could drag herself to
the door. That morning, as on any morning, she greeted me
with a radiant smile. She used to wait for me after that, sitting
in her chair by the kitchen fire, composed, the prayer book
open on her knees. Her kitchen was bare of decoration except
for two pictures. One was always a calendar from relatives
overseas. The other hung above the deal table which was
always laid with a clean white cloth for the holy sacrament. It
was a coloured photograph in a white plastic frame, and I
gazed at it for years. It was probably brought back by a friend
after a summer holiday, or it might have been a souvenir of a
trip she had made herself. I never found out because I never
asked. I would come in to her kitchen and take the little silver
pyx out of the bag that hung round my neck and lay it between
the lighted candles below the picture. For years I laid the
sacrament of the body and blood of Christ beneath that
photograph of Blackpool Tower.

At first I was rather self-consciously moved by this strange
juxtaposition. I serve a beautiful church in which High Mass
is celebrated with austere loveliness. In the sanctuary, domi-
nated by a large golden reredos, nothing tasteless or artificial

41

intrudes. For me this standard was normative. It represented the beauty and the holiness of God and the transcendent demands he made upon us. So I was moved by that picture of Blackpool Tower and the condescension of Christ who came to lie beneath it. He did not really belong there, of course. He belonged in the sanctuary, but of his great love he visited this mean dwelling and condescended to lie beneath this tasteless emblem of artificiality. Every week Christ came slumming with me. He left his golden throne and went visiting the poor, very much in the way Baron von Hügel used to make the aristocratic ladies who came to him for spiritual guidance visit the poor in the East End of London. I was moved by the condescension of Christ because I assumed there was a distance between him and this picture in its cheap Boots frame. He was the Christ of excellence, of taste, of a burning and austere holiness. He could never be the Christ of the plastic flowers and the vulgar postcards except by a supreme effort of supernatural tact.

In this way was begun my journey to the mystery of Calvary by way of Blackpool Tower. I came to realize that there was in my thinking what the philosophers call a fundamental dualism. Somehow, reality had got itself split in two. At the most obvious level there was a distance, a vast qualitative space between God and his creation. The central mystery of the faith of which I was a steward held, of course, that God himself had closed the space, had banished the distance. He had brought the two realities together in Jesus. That was the central mystery, I was sure: Jesus. In him the two had become one, so that they were no longer two, but one. Yet somehow that stubborn duality persisted. Distance remained. There was still a split and that picture of Blackpool Tower had, by accident, become emblematic of an overwhelming sense of the paradox and division that was central to the mystery of God's dealings with us. I became more and more aware that God's attitude towards us was *ambivalent*.

Of course, I cannot assert that as an absolute truth of God's nature. We only know him as he has disposed himself towards us, and we never capture even that aspect of his reality with complete clarity. Nevertheless, within the biblical revelation, which is the historical interface between God and us, I saw more and more evidence of ambivalence in God's attitude towards us. There seemed to be a terrible wrestling within him, and that struggle is dramatically represented on page after page of the Old Testament. It is seen at its crudest in the great disaster scenarios where God floods the earth because it is utterly corrupt, or where he wipes out the Cities of the Plain, or sends scorpions to chastise the Israelites wandering in the wilderness. God is *offended* by our slowness and laziness, our moral and spiritual idleness. His anger is constantly at boiling-point with us, and in constant tension with his love for us, that engulfing tenderness that also floods through the pages of the Old Testament. His anger competes with his love. His judgement wrestles with his mercy. Ambition for what we might become struggles with acceptance of what we are.

And this conflict in God seems to correspond with our experience of our own nature. Do we not spend our lives caught somewhere between the extremes of self-loathing and self-satisfaction? Is not our longing for holiness and goodness constantly modified by a strange and persistent moral inertia, our desire for life made forfeit by a constant impulse towards self-destruction? God's ambivalence towards us seems exactly mirrored in the radical ambivalence we experience in our own nature. Indeed, these two seem but different aspects of the one reality, and that reality speaks of division, of a great rent that has torn through time and its children. Every steward of the baffling mysteries of God knows this divide intimately. He knows it, first of all, in his own experience. He knows for what he stands but also bears the terrible knowledge of what he is. And he feels it acutely in his relations with those to whom he is sent. His impatience and ambition for their glorification and heroism is made weak and feeble by a terrible tenderness for them, a complete acceptance of them as they are. 'We are his people and the sheep of his pasture.' Who can expect much of sheep?

Above all, this dazzling ambiguity is seen in Jesus, the Jesus who is the mystery who makes of the two, one. Decent, liberal-minded, western Christians have so worked-over Jesus that they no longer confront him in his scandalous reality.

43

Jesus, in fact, was a spiritual terrorist. I still come across people who refuse to allow the plastic surgery of modern critical methods to remove the offence of the words of Jesus. They are shocked by his anger and cruelty, by the certainty of his conviction about hell, 'where their worm dieth not and their fire is not quenched'. In Jesus man's moral failure is taken with absolute seriousness. You sense in him a terrible urgency to call men to account by reason of the great danger they are in. He calls them to repent, to turn back before it is too late. The mystery of retribution in the message of Jesus is as unavoidable as it is unfashionable. It lashes out at us from the pages of the gospels and it has built fear and offence into Christian history. Fear, because which of us does not stand justly condemned? And offence, because which of us does not know in his heart that he is sin's victim as well as its agent?

Yet the terrible judgements of Christ and his most withering denunciations are immediately succeeded by, indeed are often co-active with, a gentleness and a heart-broken pity for us in our lostness. You sense the overwhelming force of his desire to gather us into his arms as a hen gathers her brood under her wings, and we would not. Within Jesus we find both judge and mother. We are both repelled by him and inexorably drawn towards him. To meditate on the blazing paradox of his appeal is to experience a kind of Chinese torture in which we are alternately terrified and consoled. In Jesus, somehow, we come close to total loss and total gain. We feel ourselves to be at the same time both totally rejected and utterly accepted.

'Depart from me!'
'Come unto me!'

    ...O which one? is it each one?
       That night, that year
Of now done darkness I wretch lay wrestling with (my God!)
    my God.

          (Gerard Manley Hopkins)

This mystery of gain and loss, it seems to me, is built into the very structure of Christian theology. It imparts to theology a structural ambivalence. I find this dramatically exposed in

Paul. Paul proclaims the gospel of justification by faith with desperate gratitude. He knows himself to be condemned, apart from the grace of God. Yet Paul is also the preacher of obedience and holiness who excommunicates the hapless Corinthian who is living with his father's wife. Salvation is offered without strings, but apparently we are in permanent danger of damnation! 'Which one? is it each one?'

This structural ambivalence within the mystery of God's dealing with us seems to be represented by the very dramatis personae of Christian history. The stewards of the mysteries of God seem to be either prophets or priests. The prophet seems to be the instrument of the wrath of God. He is called out to accuse people, to condemn their sin, to warn them of the great and terrible day of the Lord. When I was a young priest I wanted to be a prophet. I wanted my tongue to cut through the land like a sword. Two things happened to me. I learned that the real prophet is always reluctant. He only speaks when his heart is near to bursting. And I learned that the true prophet has no illusions about himself. I had plenty! Reinhold Niebuhr put his finger on it:

> Whenever a prophet is born, either inside or outside of the church, he faces the problem of preaching repentance without bitterness and of criticising without spiritual pride. . . . Think of sitting Sunday after Sunday under some professional holy man who is constantly asserting his egotism by criticizing yours. I would rebel if I were a layman. A spiritual leader who has too many illusions is useless. One who has lost his illusions about mankind and retains his illusions about himself is insufferable. Let the process of disillusionment continue until the self is included. At that point, of course, only religion can save from the enervation of despair. But it is at that point that true religion is born. (Reinhold Niebuhr *Leaves From The Notebook Of A Tamed Cynic*)

It is the moment of universal disillusionment, the moment of recognition of the solidarity of human sinfulness, at which the priestly task is born. For the priest comes before God with nothing left in him except a terrible pity for all men and

45

women. He is always at the point where the honest verdict has just been given, yet he pleads still for himself and for all others at that point just this side of despair. It is this task of priestly intercession which is the proper role of the Church. The Church is really the trades union of the damned.

Yet the Church is always wanting to fill the other role. It wants to be able to judge as well as plead. It wants to be able to represent both sides of the divine ambivalence. It wants to be able to represent God to man as well as man to God: on behalf of one it condemns, on behalf of the other it pleads. I know this is confusing, so let me bring it into sharper focus with a particular example: the current debate about the remarriage of the divorced. No one would pretend, I hope, that divorce is the gravest example of that human sinfulness which calls forth the anger and judgement of God. But it is bad enough, and it contradicts God's intention for us. It is one of the countless ways in which we declare our lostness. It is a part of that ungodliness and wickedness of men against which, according to Paul, God's wrath is revealed. It is a good example for us to look at because it is one of the few situations created by human sin on which the Church still has some sort of institutional leverage. In this crisis of human weakness, which side of the mystery of divine ambivalence is the Church on? Does it represent Christ the judge and divider or the Christ who would not cast the first stone? In this particular situation it really cannot do both. Whatever it might say, the victim of the situation will feel either rejected or accepted, condemned or forgiven. And it is not enough to say that the logic of Christ's teaching on marriage demands a verdict of condemnation, because there are always two logics at work in the words of Christ: the logic of damnation and the logic of forgiveness. Both are strongly present in his teaching. On what side and on whose behalf does the Church operate? I have come to believe that it is always the Church's task to plead with the divine anger on behalf of the divine mercy. I say this because I believe that this, finally, is the meaning of the mystery of Christ. Is there, then, in Christ a resolution of this conflict? Tentatively, I suggest there is. I find some hope as well as much anguish in the prophetic *failure* of Christ. I

46

cannot pretend to enter his consciousness, but I see in his mind a terrible wrestling between absolute, unconditional forgiveness and absolute, unavoidable condemnation. I have never been impressed by the speculative attempts in Christian theology to resolve this conflict, this structural ambivalence within the gospel. And I think I know why. Christ did not resolve the conflict in the abstract, with a form of words or an integrated pattern of concepts. There was no synthesis of the conflicting *logics* that drove him. He lived with that conflict, and it is mirrored in his words which both console and terrify us. In his words, however, no solution is offered. The ambiguity abides. But his words were not all that he left us. I take enormous if fearful comfort from the fact that *his words ceased*. I believe that he himself came to realize that his words alone would not do. His words could not save us, so he stopped speaking. His words ceased. The voice that entranced us with tender acceptance and withered us with towering denunciation was stilled. There was silence over all the earth. No other word was uttered except the final word of forgiveness on the cross; then there is only the living word of his dying. The angry prophet became the priest-victim. What could not be resolved he bore. What could not be reconciled in a conceptual formula he brought together on the cross.

So with fear and trembling I affirm that the last and enduring word of Christ is forgiveness, but it is not a cheap word. It is not an easy liberalizing of the terrible demand of God. That demand abides and so does our failure; and Christ brings them together in his own body on the tree. The final mystery, then, is forgiveness. The forgiveness I live by is the forgiveness I mediate. I am a steward of the forgiveness of God.

I am sure that this mystery of forgiveness must be worked through and into all the institutional patterns of our life in the Church. We must allow it to qualify the logic of our moral and institutional judgements because it is the crowning mystery of God. There is grave risk in this dangerous mystery, for some will ask, 'Is *all* to be forgiven, then?' I fear it is. I see no other way. God must forgive us or lose us.

The mystery of the cross is the final resolution of all the mysteries of God. I came to it by way of Blackpool Tower.

5. True Unbelief

Richard Harries

In the small hours of a morning in 1961 Samuel Beckett was sitting over a drink in a Paris café with Harold Pinter. Pinter suggested that Beckett's work was an attempt to impose order and form on the wretched mess mankind had made of the world, but Beckett disagreed. 'If you insist on finding form', he said, 'I'll describe it for you. I was in hospital once. There was a man in another ward, dying of throat cancer. In the silence I could hear the screams continually. That's the only kind of form my work has.'[1] What happens if we listen to those like Beckett, who hear the screams continually?

Any true sharing of minds involves listening to the other person's point of view and taking it seriously. To take it seriously means being open to the possibility of having one's own outlook modified or even radically changed by what one hears. This sets up a tension for the Christian. As 'stewards of the mysteries' we are aware of the obligation to be faithful, loyal to what God has revealed of himself. How is it possible to be loyal to what one has come to believe and at the same time genuinely open to views that contradict those beliefs?

The concept of being a steward tends to work against openness to the views of others. At the extreme, it makes people dismiss alternative views out of hand. Even in a weaker form it encourages people to listen to others without taking them seri-

1. Deirdre Bair *Samuel Beckett* Jonathan Cape 1978, p. 528

49

ously. This is not because of any deliberate discourtesy. It's just that the whole thrust of loyalty to revealed truth reinforces the tendency of sinful human beings not to take others into account, not to let the outlook of others seriously disturb one's own. Thus, taken in isolation, the notion of stewardship may be harmful. It needs to be balanced by two other values equally important to the Christian faith, love and humility. Loving someone means paying attention to what he feels and says. As Simone Weil put it,

> Not only does the love of God have attention for its sub-
> stance; the love of our neighbour, which we know to be the
> same love, is made of this same substance.... The soul
> empties itself of all its own contents in order to receive into
> itself the being it is looking at, just as he is, in all his truth.[2]

Loving someone means paying attention to what the other person is feeling and saying, and humility leads to a willingness to learn from him. It carries with it a sense that the other person may have something valuable to give, something as precious to him as our own beliefs are to us. Obviously if love and humility were present with no sense of a revealed truth to which one wanted to be faithful, there would be no tension. But in that case there would be no Christian faith either. The conclusion is that we cannot eliminate the tension between being a steward of the mysteries and being open to the truth in views opposed to one's own; we have to live with it. We could only eliminate the tension either by acting towards people of different outlook without love and humility or by having no convictions ourselves. A person will therefore be a person of the borderlands, to use a word of Professor Donald MacKinnon. The Christian will belong to one country rather than another (he is not a stateless person), he has definite beliefs and a specific commitment; but the love and humility which grow from those beliefs lead him to live on the border. He looks across at other landscapes, feeling, on occasions, their truth as his own. What Professor MacKinnon wrote of

2. Simone Weil *Waiting on God* Fontana 1959, p. 75

philosophers is applicable to all Christians: 'Because the philosopher must always be a man of the borderlands, he may perhaps feel a peculiar kinship with those who, from similarly situated territory, make protesting raids upon the theologians' cherished homeland.'[3]

In recent years many Christians have shown a more open attitude to the possibility of truth in the other religions of the world; the concept and practice of dialogue have become familiar. But exciting as it may be to discover a 'converging spirit', the more crucial and testing task of Christians is still in relation to unbelief. There is little sign in most clergy and laity of openness to unbelief, no sense that it is being listened to and taken seriously. This may be one of the main reasons that sermons are so trivial and that Christian utterances come across to the general public at no higher level than that of a party political broadcast—just something we expect people belonging to a particular group to say but with no serious relationship to the way things really are.

People give a variety of reasons for not believing in God. In the 1950s and 1960s some, influenced by linguistic philosophy, held that religious language was meaningless, or at any rate that it did not make factual assertions. Since then the careful work done by a number of Christian philosophers makes this reason for unbelief much less compelling. Indeed a recent book, *The Coherence of Christian Theism*,[4] is positively combative in its thesis that religious language is meaningful or, as Professor Swinburne prefers to put it, coherent. Then there have always been people who have argued that God's existence cannot be proved. Many Christian philosophers today would agree with this, but would add that his existence cannot be disproved either, and go on to say that the whole attempt to prove the existence of God is, from a religious point of view, inappropriate. All arguments for the existence or non-existence of God leave the matter open, and belief in God is a matter of interpreting experience one way rather than another. How one interprets experience depends upon a number of factors, including the quality of religious life that one has

3. Donald MacKinnon *Borderlands of Theology* Lutterworth 1968, p. 75
4. Richard Swinburne *The Coherence of Christian Theism* O.U.P. 1977

encountered in others, the kind of experiences one has had and one's willingness or reluctance to believe. Rational reflection and argument are only part of this process of interpretation, not the decisive factor.

Finally, there is the extent and intensity of human suffering. This has always been a difficulty for the religious mind, but there are reasons to think that the problem is more acute today than ever before. Anaesthetics and drugs spare those of us who live in the developed western world from much of the pain that previous generations could not escape. This perhaps makes us more sensitive to the suffering, particularly in others, that has not yet been eliminated. These same drugs, plus improved social conditions, enable a greater number of people to live to an old age. But this in turn makes us more aware of the indignities of old age—senility, incontinence and the sense of being useless. It might be argued that modern urban life with all its stresses causes greater mental suffering than the rooted, settled village life of a hundred years ago, even taking into account the terrible rural poverty. Then there are the reasons connected with the decline in religious belief. Even a hundred years ago the concept of heaven was very real to most people in England. This life was seen as a preparation for a better one and much suffering—including that which is, by our standards, almost unendurable, such as the loss of all the children in a family in a few weeks from typhoid—was nobly borne in the light of this belief. Now, not only has the belief in heaven faded, even for people who go to church, but progressive social policies continue to shape the climate of opinion, so that, perhaps for the first time in human history, people really believe that they can and ought to be happy. This might be a very good thing (I personally believe it is), but it does mean that when people are not happy, as is so often the case, their high expectation of happiness intensifies their misery. Finally, many of the reasons that people in the past gave as a way of coming to terms with suffering, such as the existence of the devil, God's just punishment of sinners, even God's testing of potential saints, are no longer acceptable to the majority.

We are face to face with suffering. It cannot be thought away.

Faced with suffering the 'true unbeliever' is likely to exhibit three characteristics: first, a sense of anger. The classic expression of this is by Ivan in Dostoevsky's *The Brothers Karamazov*. Under no circumstances, he argues, would it be right for a mother to forgive someone who has ordered his dogs to tear her child to pieces. 'I do not want a mother to embrace the torturer who had her child torn to pieces by his dogs! She has no right to forgive him! ... I don't want harmony. I don't want it, out of the love I bear to mankind. I want to remain with my suffering unavenged.'[5] A future state of total harmony would be morally unacceptable because it could only be brought about by a forgiveness we could not morally offer. Furthermore, no future state, however blissful, could justify the fact of children having been tortured. 'It's not God that I do not accept, Alyosha. I merely most respectfully return him the ticket.' Alyosha replies, 'This is rebellion',[6] and in his study of rebellion Camus comments that here for the first time moral truth is given priority over everything else. 'Ivan does not say that there is no truth. He says that if truth does exist it can only be unacceptable. Why? Because it is unjust. The struggle between truth and justice is brought into the open for the first time.'[7]

This sense of anger is not empty posturing for the purpose of literature. Samuel Beckett's mother was an emotional tyrant, and a large part of him was glad when she died, but as she lay dying he spent the days at her bedside. 'His nights were spent walking and talking with Geoffrey Thompson, to whom he complained bitterly of the so-called God who would permit such suffering.'[8] Earlier, when his brother Frank died, Beckett walked and talked with the same friend, 'lashing with frenzied invective at the ugliness and injustice of the world and the stupidity of God and man alike.'[9] These insights into Beckett, whom one assumes to be an agnostic, bear out the argument

---

5. Dostoevsky *The Brothers Karamazov* Penguin 1976, vol.1, p. 287
6. Something needs to be said, and can be said, to counter Ivan Karamazov. I have tried to do this in 'Ivan Karamazov's Argument' *Theology* March 1978
7. Albert Camus *The Rebel* Penguin 1962, p. 51
8. Bair, op. cit., p. 405
9. ibid., pp. 445–6

stated earlier, that it is not the alleged meaningless of Christian beliefs or the impossibility of proving the existence of God but the fact of suffering which is the most powerful factor making for disbelief in God. It's not logic but anger which makes some of the most sensitive and honest souls rebel. I once received a letter from someone who used to be a believing, practising Christian. Referring to God, it said, 'He has no kindness, no justice, no sympathy with or comprehension of the weariness and unhappiness of human life; he is a callous, indifferent, mocking, destructive tyrant—nothing more than an Amin or Ivan the Terrible on a larger scale.'

Few Christian utterances give the impression that they have grasped the strength of this moral anger. I once did a series of articles for a church newspaper. In one article I described an incident in the last war when Evelyn Waugh and F. E. Smith (later Lord Birkenhead), driven mad by the garrulousness of Randolph Churchill, took on a bet with him that he could not read the whole Bible through in a few days. Churchill accepted the challenge, but the purpose of the bet failed for he could not resist making comments, of which the most frequent was: 'God! Isn't God a shit!'[10] But when the article appeared in print, the last phrase had been changed to: 'of which the most frequent was one casting doubts on God's goodness'. Someone in the paper had felt that the readership could not cope with the thought that some people felt God was a 'shit' and had taken it upon themselves, without consulting the writer of the article, to substitute for the original a phrase in which every drop of anger had been mangled out.

The anger people feel before human suffering is not an empty gesture, a mere shaking of the fist at heaven. The anger makes the person want to do something to stop the suffering. This is the second mark of 'true unbelief': the person accepts responsibility. An emphatic No to heaven intensifies the awareness that we have to stand on our own two feet and that, if suffering is going to be reduced, it will be through human effort. In one of the Albert Camus' short stories, a ship's cook takes part in a religious procession and, because of a vow he

10. Christopher Sykes *Evelyn Waugh* Penguin 1977, p. 363

once made to God, he carries a huge stone. Suddenly he stumbles and falls. It's too heavy for him. Then an agnostic engineer who has been watching comes forward, picks up the stone and carries it himself, but not towards the temple—away, in another direction altogether. Then when he finally flings the stone down, Camus writes, 'with eyes closed he joyfully acclaimed his own strength; he acclaimed, once again, a fresh beginning in life.'[11] The story was obviously a kind of parable for Camus, in which he expressed his conviction that in the end religion is no help and we have to shoulder the burden of life ourselves. But we not only accept responsibility for our own life; we should recognize and respond to the cry of the suffering of other human beings and commit ourselves to doing something about it.

It's a thesis he worked out most movingly in the person of Dr Rieux in *The Plague*. At one point Dr Rieux is asked if he believes in God. Camus wrote:

His face still in shadow, Rieux said that he'd already answered: that if he believed in an all-powerful God he would cease curing the sick and leave that to him. But no one in the world believes in a God of that sort. . . . Anyhow, in this respect Rieux believed himself to be on the right road—in fighting against creation as he found it.[12]

Later Rieux and Father Paneloux have to spend the night listening to the death agonies of a child. Rieux lets out a burst of anger but Paneloux chides him, saying that what they witnessed was as unbearable to him as it was to the Doctor but that through grace he still managed to have faith. Rieux then says, 'It's something I haven't got; that I know. But I'd rather not discuss that with you. We're working side by side for something that unites us—beyond blasphemy and prayers. And it's the only thing that matters.' The doctor and the priest discuss further, Paneloux suggesting that Rieux too is working

11. Albert Camus, 'The Growing Stone' in *Exile and the Kingdom* Penguin 1974, p. 152
12. Albert Camus *The Plague* Penguin 1960, p. 106

for man's salvation. But the doctor insists that his concern is with man's health; this comes first. It doesn't matter whether or not he believes. "'What I hate is disease—as you well know. And whether you wish it or not, we're allies, facing them and fighting them together." Rieux was still holding Paneloux's hand. "So you see"—but he refrained from meeting the priest's eyes—'God himself can't part us now.'[13]

What comes across from this dialogue, even in its truncated form as quoted above, is the priority of human compassion over religious faith, of morality over religion. It's not that Rieux is opposed to religion, or closed to the possibility of himself believing. He is in fact open. But nothing can take priority over the task of trying to alleviate human suffering. 'It's the only thing that matters.' In their common task the priest and the doctor are united 'beyond blasphemy and prayers'. Even God himself can't part them.

The third characteristic of 'true unbelief' appears paradoxical, a contradiction of the initial moral protest against God. It consists of a sense of the worthwhileness of human endeavours, a refusal to be put down by life and a determination to make something of the opportunities it offers. The way this characteristic reveals itself in a particular person will depend upon a number of factors, not least his psychological makeup. Camus, who was forever grateful for the continuous sunshine in which he had been brought up as a child, spoke of his 'appetite for life.' It's a feeling that came across strongly in his youthful essays of 1935–6, which in later years he wanted to have reprinted, despite their clumsiness, just because they expressed something important to him which, despite everything, he had not lost. In the 1958 preface to the essays he wrote,

'There is no love of life without despair of life', I wrote, rather pompously, in these pages. I did not know at the time how right I was; I had not yet known the years of real despair. These years have come, and have managed to destroy everything in me, except, in fact, this uncontrolled

13. ibid., pp. 178–9

56

appetite for life ... the famished ardour that can be felt in these essays has never left me.[14]

In Samuel Beckett this characteristic expressed itself rather differently. Beckett had a tyrannical mother. It was only very late in life that he was able to escape her hold on him, and she left him with a crippled psyche. The line of his which more than any other sums up his emotional outlook is: 'Life is a punishment for having been born.'[15] Yet there is about Beckett a fierce integrity. The one thing that has really mattered to him is his writing. He has wanted to write something truthful about life. And he said once, 'I could not have gone through the awful wretched mess of life without having left a stain upon the silence.'[16] The phrase 'a stain upon the silence' is a typical Beckett way of speaking about, and undermining the value of, something that does in fact matter desperately to him. But it need not blind us to the fact that something has mattered to him. He has neither committed suicide nor sold out. He has kept faith to the end. In this there is some implicit recognition of the value of the human struggle.

The painter Francis Bacon has an equally bleak view of human life. In many of his paintings there seems an uncanny resemblance between human beings and slabs of raw meat at the butcher's. 'Man now realises that he is an accident, that he is a completely futile being, that he has to play out the game without reason.'[17] But despite this view of man, despite a daily consciousness of the shortness and apparent futility, not everything is futile. Something can be wrested from life in and through the struggle. Bacon says, 'My kind of psyche, it's concerned with my kind of—I'm putting it in a very pleasant way—exhilarated despair.'[18] Again, the phrase 'exhilarated despair' contains an implicit recognition that it is better to have lived than never to have lived at all. The same sense comes across in Bacon's view of art: 'We do know that our

14. Albert Camus *Selected Essays and Notebooks* Penguin 1970, p. 24
15. Samuel Beckett *For to End Yet Again and Other Fizzles* J. Calder 1976
16. Bair, op. cit., p. 640
17. David Sylvester *Interviews with Francis Bacon* Thames & Hudson 1975
18. ibid. p. 83

lives have been thickened by great art. One of the very few ways in which life has been really thickened is by the great things that a few people have left.'[19] The metaphor of thickening is used in such a way as to imply that it is better for life to be thick than thin; that the artist who through his work is helping to thicken it is engaged on something worthwhile. The wrong conclusion should not be drawn from these quotations from Camus, Beckett and Francis Bacon. No attempt is being made to say that deep down they really believe in God. There is no legerdemain being attempted. Rather, this is one of the characteristics of 'true unbelief' which the believer must listen to and taken seriously. We might think that, logically, unbelief ought to lead to total despair, but even in people who temperamentally are depressed the despair is never total. There is despair and not despair at the same time.

'True unbelief' obviously does not exist in a pure form in any one person. What has been sketched out is to some extent a composite picture. But only to some extent. The three characteristics are all present to some degree in both Camus and Beckett. The first priority of a steward of the mysteries will be to listen to such voices, really to listen, and feel the moral force, the moral persuasiveness of the views they convey. The second priority will be to say something, to reply to such voices. But how? That is the question to which all this essay leads up. How can the Christian faith be stated to people like Camus and Beckett (and these are representative figures; no doubt others could have been chosen) in such a way that it does not suffer by comparison with the moral fervour and dignity of the views it opposes? It's not simply a question of the intellectual problem of how to reconcile the existence of human suffering with a God of love.

Perhaps all that can be said has been said by people like John Hick and Austin Farrer. We can only be grateful for the work that they have done—work that is essential for a credible Christian view of existence. But it's not simply the intellectual problem. It's the moral passion and power of 'true unbelief' that has to be reckoned with. Christians have not on the whole

19. ibid p. 89

58

comprehended the fact that there are strong moral arguments against their position. They tend to assume that if Christianity isn't true, at least it is the most moral view of the world going. But this can be disputed. Alec Vidler has pointed out that it was not the rise of science or biblical criticism that turned people like George Eliot away from Christian faith. Rather, 'What it called upon them to believe, with such confidence of its superiority, struck them as morally inferior to their own ethical ideals and standards.'[20] The question then is this. Having really listened to and felt the force of voices of people like Camus and Beckett, how can the Christian faith be stated in such a way as to come across as a *morally* convincing, *morally* compelling alternative? Before human suffering, faced with a person whose anger leads him not just to protest but to commit himself to the alleviation of this suffering, a person who, despite everything, is determined to live and live with courage, what can be said?

20. Alec Vidler *The Church in an Age of Revolution* Penguin 1961, p. 113

6. Priest-Bureaucrat

Andrew Henderson

A Steward's Calling

Born into an Anglican vicar's family, with both grandfathers clergymen as well, I have felt in my bones both a keen sense of our Church's tradition and a longing and a commitment to be a faithful steward. For me, as for many priests of my generation, the authority of experience bids for attention as strongly as that of received doctrine; in my case that tension led to a vocation to combine ordination with the secular calling to statutory social work. I am fascinated by the Welfare State as a form of secular Church; in particular, the mental health field, with its ambitious claim to practise 'community care', resonated with my own experience. As a student my first conscious recognition of spiritual healing had come to me through therapeutic counselling rather than through the ministrations of the Church. It is clear to me that I am impelled along my way through an intensely personal need to stake out my own course beyond the rather suffocating pastures of family Anglicanism; I am also a creature of my times responding to the contemporary mood. I was lucky enough to have pastors round me encouraging me to take my needs seriously. Excitement still flares up in me every time I reassert that God speaks through our own needs, as through the needs of others. My stewardship, everybody's stewardship, is ourselves in sacred trust for humanity and for the coming of the kingdom of

Christ. We are called distinctively through our own constellation of needs.

The Mysteries of God

The 'of God' is important. Secular mysteries abound, and it is not long since they were called pagan. Dread and terror lurk in that word quite as much as does beatific experience. The human urge to explore will often drive us down into the subterranean depths where we can no longer see, and out into infinite spaces where our understanding peters away. All that mystery we claim in God's name. Some traditional Christian themes serve to illustrate what the phrase means to me.

Incarnation

'He came down to earth from Heaven who is God and Lord of all.' God revealed in and through humanity is a natural focus for a social worker; and statutory social work, in that it concentrates its limited resources on the most extreme forms of social and individual distress, faces us unavoidably with the catastrophic power of evil. I find myself returning to Blake's imagery of the wrestling demiurges, vividly aware of the Deceiver struggling to hold on to his kingdom of inherited pain, nameless dread and sightless eyes. Yet all of us who tread that territory are sustained and humbled by the wonder of human resilience; the power of loving expectation to evoke new life; the inexplicable will to combat and to endure.

But all that is rather vicarious; like most professionals and clergy I am a winner in society rather than a loser. For myself, I am most conscious of the mystery of the incarnation in my weaknesses and vulnerabilities rather than in my strengths. Skillful, powerful and intelligent I may be, but none of that guarantees that I am an agent of life rather than death. Overwhelmingly, I know I am called to risk, to chance my arm, in

62

following the Word made flesh in decisions and actions that may be for Christ or for the devil. Aware of mixed motives, anxiously scanning the signs, weighing alternatives, in the end I have to go on in faith, incarnating the eternal in each moment, bewildered by His changing forms; intoxicated by the Game, striving to keep up, often too exhausted to play. Whether what I do is judged to be right or wrong, whether I think I act freely or trapped in some analytic snare—all this is less important than to have acted in faith and hope and love.

Death and Resurrection

'Dying a thousand deaths a day.' It is possible to interpret the whole of life in these terms. This is made specially clear through the counselling techniques designed to help people at times of death and mourning, whether it be for someone close or for one's own approaching end. The embracing of the experience of depression and the ministry of listening and of giving attention overturn our usual sense of time and promise to be special cases of more universal truth. It is not only what we perceive to be negative; every development, every change involves the loss, the death of the past. Unless our spiritual needs are given time, as we go on we are gradually bringing ourselves to a halt through stored up hurt and distress. Often the results of this neglect are confused with the effects of age-ing. Monica Furlong chides priests who want to be social workers; I am bound to admit I do not put into practice what I clearly see: the need to overturn the inhuman pace and attitude to time engendered in our society. Whatever we are paid to do, priests are called to steward the mystery of time.

Standing back from action, while still young enough for my physical death to seem remote, the ultimate mystery of my individuality overtops everything else. My only mode of experiencing is through my separateness, even experiences of mystical union with creation and moments of transcendence. My me-ness must be at the centre of God's gift to me of myself. Yet there is a longing to go beyond this, to be delivered into a mode of being which actively transcends my separateness, rather than dissolving me like a droplet in a lake. The rare moments I have lived my life prepared to lose it, or whatever seemed then to be central to it, are the moments I have come close to the door to the Risen Life. That mysterious threshold is our goal.

Redemption and Salvation

'Loving Saviour thou didst give thine own life that we might live.' I know it must be true, but how? What on earth does it mean? I thank my God that I have never been burdened with any sense of being in touch with Jesus or God as with a person. Percolated, inspired, possessed, created—yes; but the analogy of human relationships has never been reflected in my experience of God. Perhaps clergymen's children have a particular difficulty with this imagery—in which case, I am not complaining!

The saving power of love is demonstrated in our lives daily and, dare I say it, is hardly a mystery. Such is the disenchantment with worldly power and riches, even as we still struggle for them, we know that really our humanity, our true and real selves, belong to the Kingdom of Love. In our increasingly sophisticated society, I think that is widely perceived, if not laid hold of. Is not the reason probably quite simple? In the vast history of mankind's emergence as a civilized being, it is only in these last days of internationalism and potential universal holocaust that the natural drive to survive is beginning to favour co-operation rather than naked competition. We will not overcome in the twinkling of an eye the legacy of millenia of bloody feuding for the right to survive; but to continue as a species, overcome it we must. Love becomes a secular necessity.

In the meantime, our individual behaviour is regulated by guilt. The mystery we need to lay hold of is that the guilt is borne by Another; it was never our fault in the first place. The amazing inculcation of guilt into each human infant is achieved efficiently and immediately by parents similarly deceived from the start into believing there is something basically wrong with them. The doctrine of original sin is cruelly distorted by the Deceiver as it is brought to bear on each individual, when it belongs rather at the level of creation and the cosmic Christ. Redemption is to do with laying hold of the truth that basically, naturally, we are each of us equipped to be entirely loving and co-operative, to be free and energetic in the here and now. The authority demonstrated in the life of Jesus was that he could see people as they really are and cut through the deception, fear and guilt that held them. 'He spoke as one having authority.' Stewards of this mystery ride out to the paradox of the good God who lets suffering happen.

Stewarding the Mysteries

My way into the Mysteries of God uses the categories of thought taught me by my work (see diagram p. 66).

I said I believe that the Spirit of God-made-man calls us distinctively through our needs; so in my diagram, in the lower half, each individual's interpretation is shown feeding up into the Mysteries box through the various roles and parts we play. This is a convenient shorthand, because each role draws together the complex interplay of psychological motivation and social conditioning which is implied in the upper part of the diagram.

Mysteriously speaking, the most promising parts of our lives are those which do not conform with the positive values of the world. 'How hardly shall they that are rich enter into the Kingdom of Heaven.' The conventions are too deadly. So the transformation of our vulnerable aspects seems to be at the heart of the mysteries: witness the excitement about the election of a pope who is not from the dominant western part of the Church. It is sometimes too easy to romanticize poverty or the 'little way'; it is harder to examine those aspects which are frankly despised by the current fashions of thought. In considering my own stewardship I have found myself compelled to centre on these, to my surprise.

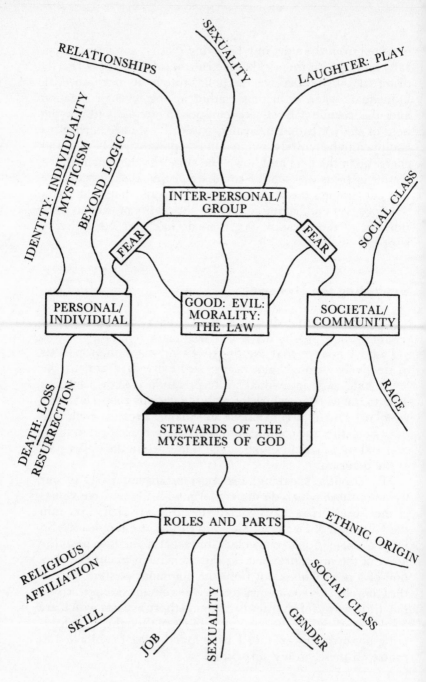

66

Even though there is a strong and positive tradition of sexual imagery in Christian mysticism, our society and the Churches within it show marked ambivalence towards sexuality, rooted no doubt in the equally strong tradition of distrust of the flesh. It is evident that the sanctified norm of the heterosexual family is now labouring under an excessive load of expectations and fantasies, often beyond its capacity to deliver. This is just as true for Christians and clergy as for society in general. As I emerged as an ordinand in my teens I came to the conclusion that I would never be able to get married; I can still remember the incredulous horror that used to rise up in me when I speculated that I probably would not grow out of the 'phase' of preferring my own sex. It seemed an unimaginable disaster, because I was trapped in a category of being that even I myself accepted as at best second-class and at worst unforgivably sinful. It was bad enough to recognize I was unlikely to get married; it was worse to live in fear and self-reproach.

Through my training I hoped that the grace of orders would resolve everything—either by creating a desire for marriage or a capacity for celibacy. In fact the Spirit seems to have led me to convert what I thought was a disability into a mainspring of my ministry and life. It is not just the pastoral work I have been able to do which confirms my goodness, nor the satisfying and happy relationships I have found with my family and friends—these have all been given to me. More precious still is the way in which this painful difference has led me to build a foundation for myself which gives me more real peace and security than any societal norms could offer. As each hurdle has been faced, I have seen more and more clearly how the devil works through fear which only Love can cast out. Though I would not want anyone to have to take on the difficulties I have had, I cannot see how else I could have been given the blessings I have received. This is not masochism but a mystery.

Working in a Bureaucracy

When I began in social work the caring element was clearly congruous with ordination; but now, as head of a social services department, I have joined the ranks of some of the most despised in our society—the bureaucrats. It is still too new for me to be very clear, but in the middle of a lot of confusion and feeling rather punch-drunk, I think I recognize the authentic signs of God's mysteries.

All big organizations evoke within their members some of the most primitive ranges of human response. Quite often I am almost overpowered in our corporate (tribal) struggles by a palpable sense of the Prince of this World, all too often catching us ordinary people up into a malign dynamic. At the same time there shines through in most of us a moving desire to reassert our loving and divine humanity within the organization. I do not believe that bureaucracy is bad in itself; like computer technology it is neutral and its application is the crux. Perhaps in our society it takes the place of the Law, the Old Covenant, providing enough stability and structure for the survival of the weak as well as the strong, and offering the opportunity for fulfilment, to go on to the New Covenant, to seek true Life. Of course bureaucracy is employed oppressively in some societies; in our own, on balance, I believe it guarantees a lot of space and freedom, not least to its detractors. Many alternative life-styles and experiments feed upon its security.

In a social services department we attract some special pressures as well as those shared by all big organizations. It seems that society is only too eager to pass over to us the expectation that we will contain, and even resolve, some of the most intractable social and personal problems; those of disaffected youth and neglected old age are the most obvious examples. The investment of resources and skills is hardly commensurate with the task, but criticism of failure is unsparing. At the same time we continually take into ourselves from our clients the aching despair and pervasive hostility of the most rejected in our communities. It is rough at the top, and it

68

is rough right through the organization. If some of us do take refuge in the bureaucratic stereotype, forgive our defensiveness and our fish-like eyes; we cannot bear to be otherwise.

I sense an immense spiritual task in awakening the thousands in our bureaucracies to the momentous and mysterious struggles of the Spirits that go on within the structures. Even more than in my home life, when beholding some unexpected resolution or triumph of humanness in the Town Hall I find upon my lips, 'My father, my father, the Chariots of Israel and the horsemen thereof!'

The Priest as Steward

Priest-workers are often challenged to explain their stance, and I say I am part of the movement to give the priesthood back to the laity. That is not to decry the place of the paid clergy but to restore a balance, and that is why I have spoken particularly from my work experience. The 1978 Reith Lectures of Dr Edward Norman argued strongly for the Church to maintain a stance ultimately over against political and secular fashions. That is difficult for the worshippers of God-made-man, but I often reflect on the unchanging essence of the mysteries of God, even though I cannot easily believe in a metaphysical Reality.

'Thou art a priest forever after the order of Melchizadek.' Priesthood has been around for a long time, but it is only in the last two hundred years that the Church has been operating in the context of anything but a bleak survival struggle for the bulk of humanity. Priests have done their part in protecting, supporting and shepherding the weak, and sometimes have attempted to curb the excesses of the strong. The mysteries of God were interpreted in the constant awareness of sudden death and the precariousness of the social order. We are now in the West living just beyond the watershed where the bulk of our population is released from preoccupation with survival and can experience more of the possibilities of human life.

69

Parental priestcraft must surely decline; yet stewards of God's mysteries are urgently needed in the new context, even if the Church is hard to stomach. To go back to an earlier theme; as the societal demand for family cohesion lessens, it is revealed what incredible fear and distress surround all forms of sexuality and personal relations. Stewards of God's mysteries should be detached from uncritical support of family life and free to add their contribution as people quest for truly responsible freedom in their relationships and living arrangements. The urgency of this for our children presses upon me. Mysteriously, the best answers are unlikely to come from the strong and the mighty.

There is a danger that the mysteries of God are more and more confined to home and neighbourhood life rather than being seen to be relevant to work. Enormous numbers of people give their best waking hours to their work; and organizations and structures are both our creations and our masters. It is frightening and exciting how dispersed power now is. It is urgent for us to claim this territory firmly for humanity just as much as home-life.

I do not argue that all change is good, but in a changing world God's stewards are free to speak with authority. That authority will be heard when it is rooted in His mysteries, for they go beyond the niceties of moral law; they are the essence of our experience of ourselves and the humanity we share with our Lord.

7. For John Ball

David Scott

Travelling from Durham on the early train
we would arrive without warning, and in no time,
you half into your cassock, there would be coffee.
If there was no reply, then either you were tired
of passing traffic; or were saying mass in church,
which was reached from the square with the plane trees,
through a parish of tenements and seedy hotels.
Your other parish was us. We came to you
because like your favourite poet Stevie Smith
you sat still; and had a private voice
which only carried as far as it needed.
News of your death came as no surprise.
I sensed that one day I would turn up
and you would not be able to rise, tiny priest,
on the one, strong, slender hand that did for two.

*John Ball died in 1978. He had been Vicar of Holy Cross, St Pancras
for eight years.*

8. The Mystery of the Transfiguration: Seven Meditations

Eric Abbott

I

'Jesus taketh with him Peter, and James and John, and leadeth them up into an high mountain apart by themselves' (Mark 9:2).

This is the divine initiative—in all our life, in all our prayer. It is prevenient grace. It is the priority of God's action. 'We love him because he first loved us' (I John 4:19). It is the divine initiative moving always towards union, towards the shared experience.

Note the little word 'with'—'we are buried with him by baptism into death'; 'we are raised with him'; 'we suffer with him'; 'we reign with him'; 'we are glorified with him'; 'we live with him'; 'Jesus taketh with him . . .' So when 'Jesus taketh with him Peter, and James and John' it is the first upward movement not only towards his own transfiguration but towards their ultimate transfiguration as well. It is the first promise that the transfigured Jesus is also the transfiguring Jesus. 'The Lord Jesus Christ shall fashion anew the body of our humiliation that it may be conformed to the body of his glory, according to the working whereby he is able even to subdue all things unto himself' (Phil.3:20–21). 'Beloved, now are we the sons of God, and it doth not yet appear what we shall

73

be: but we know that, when he shall appear, we shall be like him; for we shall see him as he is' (1 John 3:2).

'We shall be like him. . . . We shall see him as he is.' These two statements are most intimately linked, for we grow into the likeness of that at which we lovingly gaze. (The Curé d'Ars used to lean over his pulpit and say over and over again, 'We shall see him.') At the Transfiguration they saw him as he was. They were 'eye witnesses of his majesty' (2 Pet.1:16).

'Jesus taketh with him Peter, and James and John. . . .' Here is friendship—'first that which is natural'. Here is election—that mystery of all history—the chosen few; election to responsibility: 'you only have I known of all the peoples of the earth: you therefore I will punish' (Amos 3:2). Here is apostleship and training—something which they must wait to speak about till the Son of Man is risen from the dead. So it isn't simply Tom, Dick and Harry—even though Tom, Dick and Harry may and do have various transfiguring experiences, of which the greatest is love, which is rooted in the divine creation of man. They are apostles. It is therefore the beginning of the promise to transfigure Israel, to transfigure the people of God, to transfigure the Church. Be quite sure that God will never fail to go on, through history to the end, taking the Church up into the place of transfiguration, just as he also takes the Church with him into Gethsemane; and in both places Jesus is the praying Christ, and in both places Peter, and James and John, are first asleep and then awake.

'He taketh them up into a high mountain. . . .' This is the constant theme of ascending whence, first, the Redeemer has come down. He lifts up human nature ('not by conversion of Godhead into flesh but by taking manhood into God'). Prayer is the 'ascent of the mind unto God'. 'Lift up your hearts'— *sursum corda*—is the very earliest liturgical form. It is the proper view (and hence the proportion of things) which you get from the high mountain. But it is a high mountain.

'Apart by themselves . . .' This is an essential note. 'Come ye apart . . .'—not to sleep, but to be awake to the majesty of his glory. For even as he 'went up into a mountain to pray', so now we come apart to pray.

Vouchsafe to bring us, by thy grace,
To see thy glory face to face.

II

'And as he prayed the fashion of his countenance was altered.'

The Transfiguration is the feast of the praying Christ. In his prayer he entered into his glory. 'His face did shine as the sun, and his raiment was white as the light' (Matt.17:2). What sort of prayer was it? We can only answer: the prayer of union, in which the Father blesses the Son, blesses and assures him with glory. The glory is the blessing and the assurance.

Our Lord's prayer to the Father was mind to mind, heart to heart, and will to will. Here in the Transfiguration is his being at one with the Father. Our Lord prays in John 17:6: 'Glorify thou me with thine own self with the glory which I had with thee before the world was.' George Macdonald wrote: 'When he died on the Cross he did that, in the wild weather of his outlying provinces, which he had done at home in glory and gladness.' He entered into his glory so that it was visible to men.

Later on, the gospel makes us see the glory of the cross. In the end we are led to discern the glory everywhere, because it is in fact by the glory of God that we are surrounded, though discerned by faith. And we know how the Transfiguration is related to what he is going to do, to the things he must suffer. But before the Transfiguration relates to his doing, it relates to his being. The glory is always there, but there is the absolute incognito—he 'took the form of a slave'; there was 'no beauty that we should desire him' until, before these 'eye witnesses of his majesty', the glory flashes out. The meaning of it is seen in the crucifixion—the 'exodus'—and the resurrection. Transfiguration holds out the hope, the goal; but the way to it is by that radical transforming process which is represented by the cross and resurrection. We are not saved simply by 'illumination'. The way to union includes purgation. The most obvious act towards which the Transfiguration moves us is to look. (To look, even if we do not wholly see.) Look, says the Transfiguration, at what has come to pass. God has given us 'the knowledge of his glory in the face of Jesus Christ'. When we close our eyes and try to 'see Jesus', what really happens is that we see the correspondence between ourselves and the perfect image of God. His is the face of the 'proper man'—to use Martin Luther's great phrase in *Ein' Feste Burg*. ('I never set eyes on your face before', says the blind man to Jesus, who has just restored his sight in Dorothy Sayers' *The Man Born to be King*. 'Faces mean nothing to me. But you look the way you ought to look if you're the man I take you for.') But now when we see him as he is there have to be the wounds the 'glorious scars'.

There is no final contradiction between the Transfiguration and the day of the Holy Cross; and when we shall see him as he is, though then his countenance will be 'as the sun shineth in his strength' (Rev.1:16), the way taken on earth has been transfiguration, disfiguration, resurrection, ascension. He wills us to see his glory from beginning to end—glory of nativity, epiphany, crucifixion, resurrection, ascension, glory of his members at Pentecost. But there is no sure way of beholding this glory of the one Christ except the way of faith.

'Thee we adore, O *hidden* Saviour thee.' 'Verily thou art a God that hidest thyself.' But in the glorious mystery of the Transfiguration the Saviour's hidden glory—the glory he had with the Father before all worlds—stands revealed upon the holy mount.

What are the consequences of seeing his glory? First: we see the restoration of humanity—and nothing is more necessary nowadays. Second: we see the glad union of nature and supernature; the creative power of God pierces and purifies and transforms the actual creation. Third: we see the meaning of St Augustine's words concerning the Eucharist: 'Thou wilt not change me into thyself: it is thou who wilt be transformed into me.' Fourth: concerning the Church which is his Body, 'This is my beloved Son' becomes 'This is my beloved Church'. Finally: seeing his glory encourages us to contemplate.

76

III

'There talked with him Moses and Elijah, who appeared in glory' (Luke 9:30–31).

There is just that bit of danger in the joyful mystery of the Transfiguration—that we love this glory more than the glory, perceived by faith, of the disfiguration of the cross; that we contrast the two glories so as to divide rather than unite them; that we make the Transfiguration into a momentary escape from the toils and sufferings of the plain, instead of a glory which is given and received in the midst of the toils and sufferings, the mountain of vision rising out of the plain. In this way the sufferings of the present time are not forgotten on the mount but are actually the subject of heavenly converse—for they spoke of 'the decease which he should accomplish at Jerusalem'.

'I reckon that the sufferings of this present time are not worthy to be compared with the glory which shall be revealed in us', wrote St Paul in the Eighth Chapter of the Epistle to the Romans. 'For the earnest expectation of the creation waiteth for the manifestation of the sons of God.' But in the Transfiguration the glory has been revealed in us, in the very midst of the sufferings, and the Son of God has been manifested, so that we also may be sons, transfigured, changed from glory into glory. In that same eighth chapter of Romans what we are waiting for is described as 'adoption' and further defined as 'the redemption of the body'. The Transfiguration is the earnest, the promise, of the redemption of our body and of the whole of nature.

'There talked with him Moses and Elijah ...' Viewing the mystery from the side of our Lord, we may venture to say that 'as he prayed' he was meditating upon the suffering and glory of the lives of Moses and Elijah. Concerning the suffering of Moses, the Epistle to the Hebrews (11:24–27) says: (a) He chose to suffer affliction with the people of God; (b) He esteemed the reproach of Christ greater riches than the treasures of Egypt; (c) He did not fear the wrath of the king; (d) He endured as seeing him who is invisible. In the case of our Lord, how much more!

Concerning the suffering of Elijah, the First Book of Kings (chapters 18 and 19) states: (a) He is the 'troubler of Israel'; (b) He says, 'I, even I, only, remain'; (c) He says, 'O Lord, take away my life'; (d) He says, 'They seek my life, to take it away.' Jesus is uniquely the troubler—as also the Saviour—of Israel. He is left alone, except that he adds, 'yet I am not alone, because the Father is with me'. He knows that the Son of Man must suffer and tells his disciples that his enemies will kill him.

Moses had been granted a kind of transfiguration experience, a momentary and partial glimpse of the great glory. His face had shone; the veil had had to be over it for the children of Israel to bear it. Elijah also had a kind of transfiguration experience. He stood on the mount before the Lord, and there he was told what to do. Again, the deaths of Moses and Elijah were surrounded by a mysterious glory. In Moses and Elijah talking with him, Jesus received the divine assurance that the final glory could only be won in suffering, and that in that suffering he would be glorified. 'I am come forth from the Father and am come into the world: again, I leave the world, and go to the Father.' Not by transfiguration, but by suffering, death and resurrection.

If we take Moses and Elijah for our examples and apply them to our own vocations, the comments of the Epistle to the Hebrews on Moses are the very faith we require and can ask for. Elijah, in his wilderness depression, represents the natural man in us: his fear, discouragement and loneliness. But he is able to hear the still, small voice and is sent back to anoint a couple of kings and his own successor! Moses and Elijah appeared 'in glory'. The sufferings of the present time are not worthy to be compared with the glory that shall be revealed in us; and their sufferings are taken up into the eternal realm where also the sufferings of Christ are taken up, for the centre of heaven is the Lamb as it had been slain. 'If so be that we suffer with him, that we may be also glorified together.' Let, therefore, this consideration of Moses and Elijah in our Lord's Transfiguration empower and cheer us for our vocation and give us an interpretation of it.

IV

'And spake of his decease which he should accomplish at Jerusalem' (Luke 9:31).

This is the only place in the Gospels where the Greek word *exodos* is used for death. Christopher Wordsworth writes:

> Thus St. Luke appears to suggest that the death of Christ was the great moral and spiritual End to which the Law and the Prophets, represented by Moses and Elijah, looked. . . . Did not the Holy Spirit thereby intend us to infer that the Exodus, which was begun by Israel at the Red Sea, was accomplished by Christ at Jerusalem?. . . . Did he not intend us to bear in mind what was taught us by St Paul, that Christ's Exodus is the substance of which Israel's Exodus was the shadow; that Christ is the true Passover?

The Exodus was the great redemptive act of God for his people, but it was something more. It was the type and figure of the greatest event the world has ever seen: a preparation for an event which concerns all mankind until the end of time and through the countless ages of eternity; the type and figure of the world's Exodus: of mankind's deliverance by the death and passion of him who is no other than the Lord Jehovah himself, who took our nature and became incarnate; who passed through the Red Sea of his own passion and overwhelmed Satan in its abysses; who marched through that sea, and carried the world with him, and led it forth in triumph from the house of spiritual bondage—from the Egypt of Satan, sin and death—and conducted it in a glorious career towards the Canaan of its heavenly rest.

The Holy Spirit in the New Testament teaches us to regard the Exodus in this light. He teaches us that Israel was a figure of Christ, and that all things in the Exodus of Israel were figures of us; that they were figures of Christ's

Church, whose members are united together under him their Head, who had engrafted them into his own body and has made them partakers of his own death and resurrection by the sacrament of baptism, which was foreshadowed by the passage of Israel through the waters of the Red Sea. Israel's Exodus was Christ's Exodus. *(Commentary on Pentateuch p. 20)*.

Such is the rich content of meaning which we may perceive in this word 'exodus'. And this 'exodus' he is going to *accomplish*. It won't simply come. He will achieve it. That is why he can say at the end, *consummatum est*: 'It is finished'. And the death is going to be at Jerusalem. Nowhere else. Jerusalem which stones the prophets who are sent to her. 'It cannot be that a prophet perish out of Jerusalem' (Luke 13:33). 'He came unto his own, and his own received him not' (John 1:11). 'And one shall say unto him, What are these wounds in thine hands? Then he shall answer, Those with which I was wounded in the house of my friends' (Zech. 13:6).

The application of this to ourselves is a double challenge of the word 'exodus'. It is liberation *and* death. The Exodus was a historical setting free. Ask about your own liberation, your own interior freedom, through faith. (A good test of liberation is joy.) But by the grace of God I have also to achieve, accomplish, a real death—to this and that, and finally to self. Fullness of liberation will then be known. It will be the power of the resurrection in me. What death to self ought I to accomplish?

Finally, the death of our Lord accomplished at Jerusalem means that probably the real enemies are within the gates. Being wounded in the house of our friends seems so topsy turvy; but it is only an extension of the fact that in the life of the individual soul 'Ye are bidden to fight with your own selves. . . .' We tend to think that the chief sufferings should be those inflicted by the world upon the Church. Those sufferings are easy to bear compared with what tends to come upon us with greater force: the sufferings which we bear as Christians within the Church. These come because the Church is the place where the tensions of human life have to be resolved at the deepest level, and peace only comes at extreme cost: 'He made peace by the blood of his Cross' (Col.1:20). It is necessary for the Holy Spirit to speak to us often of the necessity of the death which we are to accomplish at Jerusalem.

V

'But Peter and they that were with him were heavy with sleep: and when they were awake, they saw his glory, and the two men that stood with him' (Luke 9:32). 'They were sore afraid' (Mark 9:6).

Withdrawn in distance Jesus was not. Withdrawn in another sense he was. The distance which separates us from God, because he is infinite and we are finite, is less than the distance which separates us from God because he is holy and we are sinful. This is the emphasis of the biblical writers, whereas for the philosophers it is the other way round. It is one of the insights of the men of the Bible that no man can see God and live. No wonder the reaction of the disciples was terror. It would be a mistaken pictorial representation which showed three men wrapped in adoring wonder of Jesus in glory. The symbolic representation of the ikon is correct: the disciples were completely *bouleversés*.

There are hints elsewhere in the Gospels of the disciples suddenly fearing Jesus. There is the incident in the story of the passion: 'Jesus, knowing all things that should come upon him, went forth, and said unto them, Whom seek ye? They answered him, Jesus of Nazareth. Jesus saith unto them, I am he ... As soon then as he had said unto them, I am he, they went backward, and fell to the ground' (John 18:4–6). Even on that night when he was being betrayed, they were eye-witnesses of his majesty, and in his majesty he spoke the great I AM. If this was so in the darkness of the Passion, how much more in the brightness of the Transfiguration were the sons of men struck into fear.

They were sore afraid because a cloud overshadowed them,

81

and they entered into the cloud. This is another word with both Old and New Testament allusions, and a great doctrinal meaning latent within it. We are not to think of a mist or a fog. The cloud is the glory, the Shekinah, that divine brilliance of uncreated light which is the very presence of the eternal and all-holy God. Our Lord was holding communion with that light at its very personal Source. And 'the sight of the glory of the Lord was like devouring fire on the top of the mount in the eyes of the children of Israel' (Exod. 24:17). Moses had gone up, and a cloud covered the mount; and the glory of the Lord appeared in the cloud. In later Old Testament history the cloud filled the house of the Lord. In the New Testament there is not only this cloud of Transfiguration glory, but also the cloud of the ascension when Christ returned to the glory of the heavenly places whence he had come.

The fear of the disciples is the fear of God in its highest sense: in which fear and awe are mingled with humble and adoring love and worship. This is the awe-full intimacy willed for us by our Lord, which we cannot bear—'Depart from me, for I am a sinful man, O Lord'—because of the excess of light, that light which is holiness. The cloud is almost synonymous with the glory which is the very essential attribute of God. It was the heavenly light on earth: 'Heaven and earth are full of thy glory'. In this cloud, this glory, is our human nature which God took upon himself in Christ; and here is human nature in its act of perfect adoring response. The chief end of man, 'to glorify God and enjoy him for ever', is here absolutely fulfilled in the transfigured Christ.

In the High Priestly Prayer of Jesus (John 17) Jesus prayed: 'Father, I will that they also, whom thou hast given me, be with me where I am; that they may behold my glory, which thou hast given me before the foundation of the world.' The approach to God by man, before thought so impossible—for 'he only hath immortality, dwelling in the light which no man can approach unto; whom no man hath seen, nor can see' (1 Tim. 6:16)—is made by Christ, in the prayer-union of the Transfiguration, by God to God and by man-in-God to God. The transfigured Christ in the glory of the cloud is also heaven on earth and eternity in time. The relation of time to eternity is personally shown: that time is in eternity; that this world, despite its darkness (which is of the wills of men) is in heaven. Let us steep and soak ourselves wordlessly in the sense of eternity by looking at Christ transfigured. Let us promise that space of time in which each day the remembrance of the transfigured Christ on earth will give us daily a fresh hold on the fact of eternity.

The sleep spoken of by St Luke may have been the stupor of amazement into which the disciples were struck by that excess of light which makes men as they look at Jesus, when they see him as he is—God from God, Light from Light—to be like bats looking at the sun. (At the sight of the majesty of one like unto the Son of Man St John the Divine fell at his feet as dead). We may think of their sleep as their life before conversion, *Sero te amavi*: 'Too late have I loved thee.' Yet all shall be well, for forgiveness means that God can make evil into an actual means of good. We may think of that stage of prayer in which we press against the dark cloud of the brightness of God's being, in a way for ever classically expressed by *The Cloud of Unknowing:* 'When they were awake, they saw his glory.' Let us ask to be awake, for the greatest awareness that is possible.

VI

'Peter said unto Jesus, Master, it is good for us to be here: and let us make three tabernacles; one for thee, and one for Moses, and one for Elias. For he wist not what to say' (Mark 9:5–6).

It is 'good for us to be here', because the Transfiguration lights up the essential meaning of human life and human nature; because the transfigured body of Christ is our theological and spiritual clue in the problems of faith and hope which are set us by the sufferings and chaos of the world. It is so good for us to be here that our best plan is to make three tabernacles.

The Greek word for 'tabernacle' means a bird's nest, or a tent, or both. And the regular comment on Peter's remark has much truth in it: that he wanted to stay where he was; to remain in the vision; to be close to the glory. He did not relish the exchange of the plain for the mountain. Peter is not the only one who has wanted to 'stay in the nest'. The life on the plain is a series of acts of trust, and no day can be got through without a vigorous proof of the practicality of faith as commital in trust. The Greek word for tent or booth comes from the nomadic days of Israel, when the people of God dwelt in tents. A tabernacle was therefore a movable article, less static than it sounds. It contains the idea of progress and rest. But suppose that in this sudden and bewildered statement of Peter's there is a suggestion of the Feast of Tabernacles, the connection in which the word would be most familiar to the Jew, how Peter's remark is lit up. For the Feast of Tabernacles was the Feast of In-Gathering. What Peter had seen, in a flash of faith, was the great in-gathering of the nations: the great Messianic hope purified of Jewish self-centredness. He foresaw that the kingdoms of the world would be or, rather, were the Kingdom of Christ. Whenever this vision is given, the perfect tense has to be used: 'The kingdoms of this world are become the kingdoms of our Lord, and of his Christ', not 'they will become' or 'they may become'.

Thus we are introduced at the Transfiguration to something vital to our faith: the distinction, and yet the link, between 'now' and 'not yet'. Peter, by faith, sees the in-gathering now; but we know that the in-gathering is not yet. The distinction runs through the Gospels: there is a time to be fulfilled, and before that time is 'not yet'. When the time was fulfilled Jesus 'came into Galilee preaching the kingdom of God'. He had a baptism to be baptized with—a cross to suffer—but 'My time is not yet come'. When it is come: 'Now is the Son of Man glorified, and God is glorified in him.' But on a deeper level 'not yet' refers to the fulfilled purpose of God, which requires a new heaven and a new earth. Clearly Christ is not yet King, in the sense of being acknowledged as such. In this sense the Transfiguration itself is a palpable 'not yet'. Not yet was he returned to the Father. Not yet is the death, the Exodus, which has been the subject of the converse between him and Moses and Elijah. Not yet is that resurrection which will give him a glorified body, bearing forever the marks which are the

84

credentials of the Redeemer. This 'not yet' derives not only from human imperfections but also from the very nature of human life in its necessary sequence of time, in which every generation has to learn the gospel afresh, and in which there may be a step back into barbarism if the gospel is rejected. But—in this sequence of time, in which by historical necessity nothing is complete, but everything is partial achievement, there is assurance—'Let us make three tabernacles!' 'I have seen by faith the great in-gathering of the nations: they are become the kingdoms of our Lord, and of his Christ.' It is this assurance that is asserted in the word 'now'.

This is the meaning of the miracles. All men are not yet healed; but this man is healed now. The Church is not yet perfect; but they are—at Pentecost—all filled with the Holy Ghost now. I am not yet made perfect; but I am 'saved' now. This is the gospel: though the Kingdom is not yet, it is present with power now. This is what we mean by the 'sufficient success' of the Church: that though the Kingdom tarries, it is incarnate, manifest, known to us in our experience now. Therefore 'it is good for us to be here': because in the Transfiguration the eternal is seen in its penetration into time now; and though all persons and all things are not transfigured, yet Christ being transfigured now is the earnest of all things, of the whole cosmos returned to glory. This leads us to proper hope and proper assurance. There is nothing escapist in this 'not yet' and 'now'. When we are absolved we are in the heavens now—even though the struggle continues.

This leads to creative hope. You cannot see the Transfiguration fully—with its juxtaposition and union of the natural and the supernatural; the transcendent and the immanent; God in man and man in God; the heavenly and the earthly; other-worldliness and this-worldliness; eternity and time; the vision and the cross—without receiving creative hope. The Transfiguration is 'now'; it is also 'not yet'.

The Transfiguration, crucifixion and resurrection together make a completely realistic 'Now' and 'Here'; but even they represent a 'not yet'; for not yet is God all in all. The Transfiguration is a power of creative hope which 'maketh not ashamed'. Some hopes—like Utopia—'make ashamed'. The

Kingdom of God, built upon the incarnation, transfiguration, crucifixion, resurrection and ascension, does not make ashamed. It is real. It takes account of everything in the heights and depths of human nature. So we live in the vision of the in-gathering, but in hope: between the beginning and the end—'in the beginning God'; in the End, God shall be all in all; 'between the times', with always a 'not yet', but always, in response to faith, a 'now', a present blessing, a present assurance.

We are isolated, unsuccessful; we get sorrowful about the Church. We feel that mankind is imprisoned in its own works. But we unite ourselves with the humiliated Jesus, knowing that the humiliated Jesus and the ascended Jesus are one Christ. And just when we think we are imprisoned in our own works, the Word of God breaks in; there is a fresh descent of the Dove, and creative possibilities are opened up.

'Where, Lord?' Here and there. Where there is faith. But 'when the Son of Man cometh, shall he find faith on the earth?' Shall he find Christians patient enough in the ambiguities of history, patient with the 'not yet' but sure of the 'now'?

VII

'And there came a voice out of the cloud, saying, This is my beloved Son: hear him' (Luke 9:35). 'They saw no man any more, save Jesus only with themselves' (Mark 9:8).

The Transfiguration story ends with a direct command from the glory to the disciples—a statement of fact, and a command: 'This is my beloved Son: hear him.' How do they fare? Not very well just yet. The glory is not yet imparted to them. They have been afraid. They are commanded to silence. But they have seen, and they can remember. And then come all those terrible experiences, from the Transfiguration to the day when our Lord went up the steeper hill of Calvary, until in the end his corpse is laid in the tomb.

86

It is our Lord's will to share his glory. It is he who, in the New Testament phrase, 'brings many sons to glory'; but, then and now, it is on the further side of the crucifixion that the glory is given and imparted. It was after the Cross, after Pentecost, after conversion that Stephen's face was seen 'as it had been the face of an angel' and that as he 'looked up steadfastly into heaven he saw the glory of God'.

The Transfiguration which we desire is not without pain and sweat. This change from glory to glory is through death, as we let ourselves go more and more. All that the Transfiguration has anticipated—for the Transfiguration is a great anticipation—is given to us in full measure when we have passed through our own (spiritual) grave and gate of death. We have to assume therefore a real conversion before we can be sure that the Transfiguration can be used for our soul's advance. But then, when it comes to us in our mind and memory, after Good Friday, and Easter, and Pentecost—as it remained in the memory of Peter, James and John, though they were not immediately partakers of the Transfiguration glory—it leads right on to the prayer of union; and, when combined with a lively trust in the Holy Spirit, it leads to the imparted likeness to our Lord which is God's will for us: an imparted likeness through contemplation. 'We shall be like him ... we shall see him as he is ... This is my beloved Son ... These are my beloved sons.'

The Transfiguration is the promise of the family likeness in the household of God. We become like that which we love. We become like him whom we love. Because we are 'bound up in the bundle of life' with other men, this is the greatest thing we can do for them: to be transfigured by the transfiguring Christ. Loving him, seeing him, hearing him, we become like him; as we pray, if we really believe in the Holy Spirit's power to make us what we are not, the fashion of our countenance is altered. In face alone St Paul noted something different in the expression of Christians, for they 'reflect as in a mirror the glory of the Lord'. And this is no superficial thing, for the natural self is being changed into the new spiritual self: 'as we have borne the image of the earthly, we shall also bear the image of the heavenly'. And this is no sentimental or emotional thing: 'Be ye transformed by the renewing of your mind', says St Paul; and we may think thankfully how God has begun to do this already.

'This is my beloved Son: hear him.' He is God's beloved Son, by whose tranfigured and risen body you are given your clue to life. Hear him, and by faith cleave to him, despite all difficulties. He is the beloved Son. We are God's sons in the Son. His Transfiguration means that it 'doth not yet appear what we shall be'.

'Hear him.' Our fundamental spiritual exercise is to practise his presence. 'They saw no man any more, save Jesus only with themselves.'